Postcolonial theory

Interior of Tuncum, Madurai by Edmund David Lyon, Prints and Drawings Section of the Oriental and India Office Collections, British Library (OIOC photo 1001 [2975])

Postcolonial Theory

A Critical Introduction

Leela Gandhi

Columbia University Press
New York

For Indu Gandhi and Julia Briggs

Columbia University Press
Publishers Since 1893
New York   Chichester, West Sussex
Copyright © 1998 Leela Gandhi

First published in 1998 by Allen & Unwin in Australia

Library of Congress Cataloging-in-Publication Data

Gandhi, Leela, 1966–
    Postcolonial theory : a critical introduction / Leela Gandhi.
    p. cm.
    Includes bibliographical references and index.
    ISBN 0-231-11272-6 (alk. paper). — ISBN 0-231-11273-4
    (pbk. : alk. paper)
    1. Postcolonialism. I. Title.
JV51.G36   1998
320.9′09′045—dc21   97-32402
                                                         CIP

Printed in Singapore by KHL Printers

p 10 9 8 7 6 5 4 3 2

Contents

Acknowledgments

I wish to thank my colleagues at the School of English, La Trobe University, for their patience and support, and Elizabeth Weiss and others at Allen & Unwin for their advice and enthusiasm. Thanks also to Dipesh Chakrabarty who gave me access to his work and helped to shape ideas, to David Lloyd whose writing, likewise, offered crucial insights into the 'problem' of anti-colonial nationalisms, and to Ruth Vanita whose polemical and stimulating resistance to the claims of postcolonial theory finds utterance in the 'critique' aspect of this book.

I have gained enormously from conversations with Marion Campbell, Joanne Finkelstein, Raju Pandey and Sanjay Seth, who were generous with their time and friendship. To Bronte Adams I owe profound thanks for her reservoir of faith and encouragement; she brought, as always, both pleasure and perspective to the activity of reading and writing.

My greatest debt is to Pauline Nestor, who read through this manuscript and its drafts with care and patience. I learnt much from her editorial and critical interventions, and her hospitality and support considerably eased the rough passage of this book.

Preface

In the last decade postcolonialism has taken its place with theories such as poststructuralism, psychoanalysis and feminism as a major critical discourse in the humanities. As a consequence of its diverse and interdisciplinary usage, this body of thought has generated an enormous corpus of specialised academic writing. Nevertheless, although much has been written under its rubric, 'postcolonialism' itself remains a diffuse and nebulous term. Unlike Marxism or deconstruction, for instance, it seems to lack an 'originary moment' or a coherent methodology. This book is an attempt to 'name' postcolonialism—to delineate the academic and cultural conditions under which it first emerged and thereby to point to its major preoccupations and areas of concern.

There are correspondingly two parts to the book—the first offers an account of postcolonialism's academic and intellectual background, and the second elaborates the themes and issues which have most engaged the attention of postcolonial critics. In the main, the intellectual history of postcolonial theory is marked by a dialectic between Marxism, on the one hand, and poststructuralism/postmodernism, on the other. So, too, this theoretical contestation informs the academic content of postcolonial analysis, manifesting itself in an ongoing debate between the competing claims of nationalism and internationalism, strategic essentialism and hybridity, solidarity and dispersal, the politics of structure/totality and the politics of the fragment.

Critics on both sides of this divide are persuasive in their claims, and compelling in their critique of theoretical opponents. Neither the assertions of Marxism nor those of poststructuralism, however, can exhaustively account for the meanings and consequences of the colonial encounter. While the poststructuralist critique of Western epistemology and theorisation of cultural alterity/difference is indispensable to postcolonial *theory*, materialist philosophies, such as Marxism, seem to supply the most compelling basis for postcolonial *politics*. Thus, the postcolonial critic has to work toward a synthesis of, or negotiation between, both modes of thought. In a sense, it is on account of its commitment to this project of theoretical and political integration that postcolonialism deserves academic attention.

Finally, there is the question of postcolonialism's constituency—the cultural audience for whom its theoretical disquisitions are most meaningful. In my reading of this field, there is little doubt that in its current mood postcolonial theory principally addresses the needs of the Western academy. It attempts to reform the intellectual and epistemological exclusions of this academy, and enables non-Western critics located in the West to present their cultural inheritance as knowledge. This is, of course, a worthwhile project and, to an extent, its efforts have been rewarded. The Anglo-American humanities academy has gradually stretched its disciplinary boundaries to include hitherto submerged and occluded voices from the non-Western world. But, of course, what postcolonialism fails to recognise is that what counts as 'marginal' in relation to the West has often been central and foundational in the non-West. Thus, while it may be revolutionary to teach Gandhi as political theory in the Anglo-American academy, he is, and has always been, canonical in India. Despite its good intentions, then, postcolonialism continues to render non-Western knowledge and culture as 'other' in relation to the normative 'self' of Western epistemology and rationality. Rarely does it engage with the theoretical self-sufficiency of African, Indian, Korean, Chinese knowledge systems, or foreground those cultural and historical conversations which circumvent the Western world.

Nowhere is this book motivated by a desire for postcolonial revenge. It does not seek finally to marginalise the West—to render it an excluded and uneasy eavesdropper to cryptic exchanges between, for instance, Africa and India. Its manifesto, if any, is this: that postcolonialism diversify its mode of address and learn to speak more adequately to the world which it speaks for. And, in turn, that it acquire the capacity to facilitate a democratic colloquium between the antagonistic inheritors of the colonial aftermath.

1

After colonialism

In 1985 Gayatri Spivak threw a challenge to the race and class blindness of the Western academy, asking 'Can the subaltern speak?' (Spivak 1985). By 'subaltern' Spivak meant the oppressed subject, the members of Antonio Gramsci's 'subaltern classes' (see Gramsci 1978), or more generally those 'of inferior rank', and her question followed on the work begun in the early 1980s by a collective of intellectuals now known as the Subaltern Studies group. The stated objective of this group was 'to promote a systematic and informed discussion of subaltern themes in the field of South Asian studies' (Guha 1982, p. vii). Further, they described their project as an attempt to study 'the general attribute of subordination in South Asian society whether this is expressed in terms of class, caste, age, gender and office or in any other way' (Guha 1982, p. vii). Fully alert to the complex ramifications arising from the composition of subordination, the Subaltern Studies group sketched out its wide-ranging concern both with the visible 'history, politics, economics and sociology of subalternity' and with the occluded 'attitudes, ideologies and belief systems—in short, the culture informing that condition' (Guha 1982, p. vii). In other words, 'subaltern studies' defined itself as an attempt to allow the 'people' finally to speak within the jealous pages of elitist historiography and, in so doing, to speak for, or to sound the muted voices of, the truly oppressed.

Spivak's famous interrogation of the risks and rewards which haunt any academic pursuit of subalternity drew attention to the complicated relationship between the knowing investigator and the (un)knowing subject of subaltern histories. For how, as she queried, 'can we touch the consciousness of the people, even as we investigate their politics? With what voice-consciousness can the subaltern speak?' (Spivak 1988 [1985], p. 285). Through these questions Spivak places us squarely within the familiar and troublesome field of 'representation' and 'representability'. How can the historian/investigator avoid the inevitable risk of presenting herself as an authoritative representative of subaltern consciousness? Should the intellectual 'abstain from representation?' (Spivak 1988 [1985], p. 285) Which intellectual is equipped to represent which subaltern class? Is there an 'unrepresentable subaltern class that can know and speak itself?' (Spivak 1988 [1985] p. 285) And finally, who—if any—are the 'true' or 'representative' subalterns of history, especially within the frame of reference provided by the imperialist project?

The complex notion of subalternity is pertinent to any academic enterprise which concerns itself with historically determined relationships of dominance and subordination. Yet it is postcolonial studies which has reponded with the greatest enthusiasm to Spivak's 'Can the subaltern speak?'. Utterly unanswerable, half-serious and half-parodic, this question circulates around the self-conscious scene of postcolonial texts, theory, conferences and conversations. While some postcolonial critics use it to circumscribe their field of enquiry, others use it to license their investigations. And, above all, the ambivalent terrain of subaltern-speak has given rise to a host of competing and quarrelsome anti- and postcolonial subalternities. There is little agreement within postcolonial studies about the worst victims of colonial oppression, or about the most significant anti-colonial insurgencies. Metropolitan South Asian, African and West Indian poststructuralists battle Marxists at home; mainstream intellectuals within 'settler' colonies struggle against the claims of indigenous intellectuals and representatives; and feminist critics contest the masculinist evasions of nationalist historiography. Thus, while Spivak concluded her provocative essay by categorically insisting that 'the subaltern cannot speak' (Spivak 1988 [1985], p. 308), postcolonial studies has come to represent a confusing and often unpleasant babel of subaltern voices. How then, can we begin to make sense of—or, indeed, take sense from—this field?

Over the last decade, postcolonial studies has emerged both as a meeting point and battleground for a variety of disciplines and theories. While it has enabled a complex interdisciplinary dialogue within the humanities, its uneasy incorporation of mutually antagonistic theories—such as Marxism and poststructuralism—confounds any uniformity of approach. As a consequence, there is little consensus regarding the proper content, scope and relevance of postcolonial studies. Disagreements arising from usage and methodology are reflected in the semantic quibbling which haunts attempts to name postcolonial terminology. Whereas some critics invoke the hyphenated form 'post-colonialism' as a decisive temporal marker of the decolonising process, others fiercely query the implied chronological separation between colonialism and its aftermath—on the grounds that the postcolonial condition is inaugurated with the onset rather than the end of colonial occupation. Accordingly, it is argued that the unbroken term 'postcolonialism' is more sensitive to the long history of colonial consequences.

On a different though related note, some theorists have announced a preference for the existential resonance of 'the postcolonial' or of 'postcoloniality' over the suggestion of academic dogma which attaches to the notion of postcolonial-*ism*. In the main, the controversy surrounding postcolonial vocabulary underscores an urgent need to distinguish and clarify the relationship between the material and analytic cognates of postcolonial studies. In its more self-reflexive

3

moments, postcolonial studies responds to this need by postu-lating itself as a theoretical attempt to engage with a particular historical condition. The theory may be named 'postcolonial-ism', and the condition it addresses is best conveyed through the notion of 'postcoloniality'. And, whatever the controversy surrounding the theory, its value must be judged in terms of its adequacy to conceptualise the complex condition which attends the aftermath of colonial occupation.

In this chapter I will examine some dimensions of, and possibilities for, the relationship between postcoloniality and postcolonialism in terms of the decolonising process. The emergence of anti-colonial and 'independent' nation-States after colonialism is frequently accompanied by a desire to forget the colonial past. This 'will-to-forget' takes a number of historical forms, and is impelled by a variety of cultural and political motivations. Principally, postcolonial amnesia is symptomatic of the urge for historical self-invention or the need to make a new start—to erase painful memories of colonial subordination. As it happens, histories, much as fam-ilies, cannot be freely chosen by a simple act of will, and newly emergent postcolonial nation-States are often deluded and unsuccessful in their attempts to disown the burdens of their colonial inheritance. The mere repression of colonial memories is never, in itself, tantamount to a surpassing of or emancipa-tion from the uncomfortable realities of the colonial encounter.

In response, postcolonialism can be seen as a theoretical resistance to the mystifying amnesia of the colonial aftermath. It is a disciplinary project devoted to the academic task of revisiting, remembering and, crucially, interrogating the colo-nial past. The process of returning to the colonial scene discloses a relationship of reciprocal antagonism and desire between coloniser and colonised. And it is in the unfolding of this troubled and troubling relationship that we might start to discern the ambivalent prehistory of the postcolonial condition. If postcoloniality is to be reminded of its origins in colonial oppression, it must also be theoretically urged to recollect the compelling seductions of colonial power. The forgotten archive

4

of the colonial encounter narrates multiple stories of contestation and its discomfiting other, complicity.

In addition, the colonial archive preserves those versions of knowledge and agency produced in response to the particular pressures of the colonial encounter. The colonial past is not simply a reservoir of 'raw' political experiences and practices to be theorised from the detached and enlightened perspective of the present. It is also the scene of intense discursive and conceptual activity, characterised by a profusion of thought and writing about the cultural and political identities of colonised subjects. Thus, in its therapeutic retrieval of the colonial past, postcolonialism needs to define itself as an area of study which is willing not only to make, but also to gain, theoretical sense out of that past.

The colonial aftermath

The colonial aftermath is marked by the range of ambivalent cultural moods and formations which accompany periods of transition and translation. It is, in the first place, a celebrated moment of arrival—charged with the rhetoric of independence and the creative euphoria of self-invention. This is the spirit with which Saleem Sinai, the protagonist of Salman Rushdie's *Midnight's Children*, initially describes the almost mythical sense of incarnation which attaches to the coincidence of his birth and that of the new Indian nation on the momentous stroke of the midnight hour on 15 August 1947: 'For the next three decades, there was to be no escape. Soothsayers had prophesied me, newspapers celebrated my arrival, politicos ratified my authenticity' (Rushdie 1982, p. 9). Predictably, and as Rushdie's Indian Everyman, Saleem Sinai, ultimately recognises, the colonial aftermath is also fraught by the anxieties and fears of failure which attend the need to satisfy the historical burden of expectation. In Sinai's words, 'I must work fast, faster than Scheherazade, if I am to end up meaning—yes, meaning—something. I admit it: above all things, I fear absurdity' (Rushdie 1982, p. 9). To a large extent, Saleem Sinai's obsessive 'creativity' and semantic profusion is fuelled by his apprehension that the inheritors of the colonial aftermath must in some sense instantiate a totally new world. Saleem Sinai's tumble into independent India is, after all, framed by the crippling optimism of Nehru's legendary narration of postcoloniality: 'A moment comes, which comes but rarely in history, when we step out from the old to the new; when an age ends; and when the soul of a nation long suppressed finds utterance . . .' (Rushdie 1982, p. 116).

To quote Jameson's observations on postmodernism out of context, we might say that the celebratory cyborg of postcoloniality is also plagued by 'something like an imperative to grow new organs, to expand our sensorium and our body to some new, yet unimaginable, perhaps impossible, dimensions' (Jameson 1991, p. 39). In pursuing this imperative, however, postcoloniality is painfully compelled to negotiate the contradictions arising from its indisputable historical belatedness, its *post*-coloniality, or political and chronological derivation from colonialism, on the one hand, and its cultural obligation to be meaningfully inaugural and inventive on the other. Thus, its actual moment of arrival—into independence— is predicated upon its ability to successfully imagine and execute a decisive departure from the colonial past.

Albert Memmi, the Tunisian anti-colonial revolutionary and intellectual, has argued that the colonial aftermath is fundamentally deluded in its hope that the architecture of a new world will magically emerge from the physical ruins of colonialism. Memmi maintains that the triumphant subjects of this aftermath inevitably underestimate the psychologically tenacious hold of the colonial past on the postcolonial present. In his words: 'And the day oppression ceases, the new man is supposed to emerge before our eyes immediately. Now, I do not like to say so, but I must, since decolonisation has demonstrated it: this is not the way it happens. The colonised lives for a long time before we see that really new man' (Memmi 1968, p. 88).

Memmi's political pessimism delivers an account of postcoloniality as a historical condition marked by the visible apparatus of freedom and the concealed persistence of unfree-dom. He suggests that the pathology of this postcolonial limbo between arrival and departure, independence and dependence, has its source in the residual traces and memories of subordi-nation. The perverse longevity of the colonised is nourished, in part, by persisting colonial hierarchies of knowledge and value which reinforce what Edward Said calls the 'dreadful secondariness' (Said 1989, p. 207) of some peoples and cul-tures. So also the cosmetic veneer of national independence barely disguises the foundational economic, cultural and polit-ical damage inflicted by colonial occupation. Colonisation, as Said argues, is a 'fate with lasting, indeed grotesquely unfair results' (1989, p. 207).

In their response to the ambiguities of national inde-pendence, writers like Memmi and Said insist that the colonial aftermath does not yield the end of colonialism. Despite its discouraging tone, this verdict is really framed by the quite benign desire to mitigate the disappointments and failures which accrue from the postcolonial myth of radical separation from Europe. The prefix 'post', as Lyotard has written, elab-orates the conviction 'that it is both possible and necessary to break with tradition and institute absolutely new ways of living and thinking' (Lyotard 1992, p. 90). Almost invariably, this sort of triumphant utopianism shapes its vision of the future out of the silences and ellipses of historical amnesia. It is informed by a mistaken belief in the immateriality and dis-pensability of the past. In Lyotard's judgment, 'this rupture is in fact a way of forgetting or repressing the past, that is to say, repeating it and not surpassing it' (Lyotard 1992, p. 90). Thus, we might conclude that the postcolonial dream of discontinuity is ultimately vulnerable to the infectious residue of its own unconsidered and unresolved past. Its convalescence is unnecessarily prolonged on account of its refusal to remem-ber and recognise its continuity with the pernicious malaise of colonisation.

If *postcoloniality* can be described as a condition troubled by the consequences of a self-willed historical amnesia, then the theoretical value of *postcolonialism* inheres, in part, in its ability to elaborate the forgotten memories of this condition. In other words, the colonial aftermath calls for an ameliorative and therapeutic theory which is responsive to the task of remembering and recalling the colonial past. The work of this theory may be compared with what Lyotard describes as the psychoanalytic procedure of *anamnesis*, or analysis—which urges patients 'to elaborate their current problems by freely associating apparently inconsequential details with past situations—allowing them to uncover hidden meanings in their lives and their behaviour' (Lyotard 1992, p. 93). In adopting this procedure, postcolonial theory inevitably commits itself to a complex project of historical and psychological 'recovery'. If its scholarly task inheres in the carefully researched retrieval of historical detail, it has an equally compelling political obligation to assist the subjects of postcoloniality to live with the gaps and fissures of their condition, and thereby learn to proceed with self-understanding.

Salman Rushdie sheds light on this necessity in a wonderful moment of betrayal and reconciliation in *Midnight's Children*, when the anti-hero and narrator, Saleem Sinai, reveals the cultural miscegenation and comic misrecognition of his celebrated birth. Early in the novel, and at the same time as Amina Sinai struggles to produce her child in Dr Narlinkar's Nursing Home, a poor woman called Vanita suffers a neglected labour in the 'charity ward'. The child she is about to bear is the unexpected consequence of an affair with an Englishman, William Methwold, who boasts direct descent from a particularly imperialistic East India Company officer. When these children are finally delivered, a somewhat crazed midwife called Mary Pereira switches Amina's and Vanita's babies around. Thus, Saleem Sinai, hailed by Nehru himself as the child of independent India, is really the son of a reluctantly departing coloniser. But this accident, as the adult Saleem insists, is the allegorical condition of all those who inherit the colonial aftermath: 'In fact, all over the new India, the dream we all shared, children were being born who were only partially the offspring of their parents' (Rushdie 1982, p. 118). In his digressive self-narration, Saleem Sinai simultaneously refuses the guilt of unauthenticity and the desire to withhold the knowledge of his flawed genealogy. The Sinais, we are told, eventually reconcile themselves to the fact of Methwold's bloodline, namely, to the hybrid inadequacies of their own postcoloniality. As Saleem explains: 'when we eventually discovered the crime of Mary Pereira, we all found that it *made no difference*! I was still their son: they remained my parents. In a kind of collective failure of imagination, we learned that we simply could not think our way out of our pasts . . .' (Rushdie 1982, p. 118). We might modify this narrative wisdom slightly to say that, perhaps, the only way out is by thinking, rigorously, *about* our pasts.

Postcolonial re-membering

In his comments on Frantz Fanon's *Black Skin, White Masks*, the postcolonial critic, Homi Bhabha, announces that memory is the necessary and sometimes hazardous bridge between colonialism and the question of cultural identity. Remembering, he writes, 'is never a quiet act of introspection or retrospection. It is a painful re-membering, a putting together of the dismembered past to make sense of the trauma of the present' (Bhabha 1994, p. 63). Bhabha's account of the therapeutic agency of remembering is built upon the maxim that memory is the submerged and constitutive bedrock of conscious existence. While some memories are accessible to consciousness, others, which are blocked and banned—sometimes with good reason—perambulate the unconscious in dangerous ways, causing seemingly inexplicable symptoms in everyday life. Such symptoms, as we have seen, can best be relieved when the analyst—or, in Bhabha's case the theorist—releases offending memories from their captivity. The procedure of analysis–theory, recommended here, is guided by Lacan's ironic reversal of the Cartesian *cogito*, whereby the rationalistic truth of 'I think therefore I am' is rephrased in the proposition: 'I think where I am not, therefore I am where I do not think' (Lacan 1977, p. 166).

9

In the process of forging the reparative continuity between cultural identity and the historical past, the theorist/analyst is also required to recognise the qualitative difference between two types of amnesia. The mind, as both Freud and Lacan maintain, engages in either the better known neurotic 'repression'—*Verdrängung*—of memory; or, and more devastatingly in its psychotic 'repudiation'—*Verwerfung* (see Bowie 1991, pp. 107–9). If the activity of *Verdrängung* censors and thereby disguises a vast reservoir of painful memories, the deceptions of *Verwerfung* tend to transform the troublesome past into a hostile delirium. The memories and images expelled through the violence of repudiation enter into what Lacan describes as a reciprocal and 'symbolic opposition to the subject' (Lacan 1977, p. 217). These phantasmic memories thus become simultaneously alien, antagonistic and unfathomable to the suffering self.

To a large extent, the colonial aftermath combines the obfuscations of both *Verdrängung* and *Verwerfung*. Its unwillingness to remember what Bhabha describes as the painful and humiliating 'memory of the history of race and racism' (Bhabha 1994, p. 63) is matched by its terrified repudiation and utopian expulsion of this past. In response, the theoretical re-membering of the colonial condition is called upon to fulfil two corresponding functions. The first, which Bhabha foregrounds as the simpler disinterment of unpalatable memories, seeks to uncover the overwhelming and lasting violence of colonisation. The second is ultimately reconciliatory in its attempt to make the hostile and antagonistic past more familiar and therefore more approachable. The fulfilment of this latter project requires that the images expelled by the violence of the postcolonial *Verwerfung* be reclaimed and owned again. This is, of course, another way of saying that postcoloniality has to be made to concede its part or complicity in the terrors—and errors—of its own past. In Sara Suleri's words: 'To tell the history of another is to be pressed against the limits of one's own—thus culture learns that terror has a local habitation and a name' (Suleri 1992, p. 2).

Thus, we might conclude that the forgotten content of postcoloniality effectively reveals the story of an ambivalent and symbiotic *relationship* between coloniser and colonised. Accordingly, the reparative proddings of postcolonial theory/analysis are most successful when they are able to illuminate the contiguities and intimacies which underscore the stark violence and counter-violence of the colonial condition. Albert Memmi has argued that the lingering residue of colonisation will only decompose if, and when, we are willing to acknowledge the reciprocal behaviour of the two colonial partners. The colonial condition, he writes, 'chained the coloniser and the colonised into an implacable dependence, moulded their respective characters and dictated their conduct' (Memmi 1968, p. 45). Memmi's predication of this perverse mutuality between oppressor and oppressed is really an attempt to understand the puzzling circulation of desire around the traumatic scene of oppression. The desire of the coloniser for the colony is transparent enough, but how much more difficult it is to account for the inverse longing of the colonised. How, as Memmi queries, 'could the colonised deny himself so cruelly . . . How could he hate the colonisers and yet admire them so passionately?' (1968, p. 45)

This situation of hate and desire described by Memmi poses a problem for 'oppositional' postcolonial theory, which scavenges the colonial past for what Benita Parry describes as an 'implacable enmity between native and invader' (Parry 1987, p. 32). The aim of this combative project is to promote, in Parry's words, 'the construction of a politically conscious, unified revolutionary Self, standing in unmitigated opposition to the oppressor' (p. 30). In fact, the colonial archive mitigates these simple dichotomies through its disclosure of the complicating logic and reciprocity of desire. It shows that the colonised's predicament is, at least partly, shaped and troubled by the compulsion to return a voyeuristic gaze upon Europe. How should we as theorists respond to this gaze? How does it fit into the theoretical economy of combat and enmity? We might gesture toward some answers by saying that the battle lines *between* native and invader are also replicated *within*

11

native and invader. And—as Memmi might say—the crisis produced by this self-division is at least as psychologically significant as those which attend the more visible contestations of coloniser and colonised.

There is a savage account of such postcolonial schizophrenia in Vikram Seth's epic novel, A *Suitable Boy* (1993). The impossibly home-grown, or *desi*, shoemaker hero, Haresh, is attempting to impress his suitability upon the heroine's obnoxious Anglophile brother, Arun Mehra, who has just been holding forth about the singular joys of Hamely's toy shop. Mehra claims to know the exact location of Hamley's, 'on Regent Street, not far from Jaeger's'. And yet, when Haresh—of the brown-and-white co-respondent shoes—politely inquires when the Mehras were last in the imperial capital, we discover that they have never been to London. There is an awful pause, long enough for our readerly sympathies to attach themselves firmly on the side of the shoemaker, before Arun splutters, 'but of course we're going in a few months time'. Seth's harsh satire on the Arun Mehras exploits the stigma of unauthenticity which haunts the 'Orient's' longing for its conquering other. And yet, there is a pathos even in the Mehras' excessive Anglophilia. Homi Bhabha might say that they are ideologically interpellated by the restrictive confinement of knowledge and value to the sovereign map of Europe. The Europe they know and value so intimately is always elsewhere. Its reality is infinitely deferred, always withheld from them. Worse still, their questing pursuit of European plenitude, their desire to own the coloniser's world, requires a simultaneous disowning of the world which has been colonised. Arun Mehra can only sustain his apprentice brown-sahibship by speaking in the language of his conquerors. A hard day in the office produces the following ruminations: 'The British knew how to run things . . . they worked hard and they played hard. They believed in command, and so did he . . . What was wrong with this country was a lack of initiative. All the Indians wanted was a safe job. Bloody pen pushers, the whole lot of them' (Seth 1993, p. 422). And so Arun Mehra loses the respect of his author and his readers.

A more sympathetic gloss on the Mehras might suggest that their postcolonial investment in Europe is also accompanied by a progressive, and ultimately crippling, loss of 'home'. In an early poem called 'Diwali', Seth offers a literary preamble to the Mehras through a considerably more sympathetic self-portrait (Seth 1994). This poem too considers the deleterious effects of a colonial education—but with a greater sense of the irresistible literary and cultural temptations of Europe. Its ambivalent apotheosis to 'Englishness' enacts what Ashis Nandy has eloquently described as the 'intimate enmity' of the colonial condition (Nandy, 1983). Seth's poem is spoken from a cultural crossing where the privileges and passions attached to the magic of 'English' literature are constantly undone and unworked by an underlying sense of cultural transgression. Traversing the genealogy of a Punjabi family from rural self-sufficiency to colonised civility, 'Diwali' chronicles the effort it takes for six generations of Punjabi peasants to finally gain 'the conqueror's authoritarian seal', by sending 'a son to school' (Seth 1994 [1981], p. 64). Suddenly, family history is rewritten as a faltering generational progress into coloniality. The crisis turns on the paradox that what is eminently desirable through Englishness—'a job . . . power'—is also, and at the same time, rendered utterly undesirable, once again, through the taint of 'snobbery, the good life' (1994 [1981], p. 65) Likewise, and perhaps more painfully, the etymology of the language that is loved so intimately by the poet belongs elsewhere and at a distance, to another—sometimes hostile and abusive—'tongue'. This younger Seth ponders the impossibility of crawling, willingly, beside the 'meridian names' of the English poets 'Jonson, Wordsworth', in the face of Macaulay's prophesy: 'one taste / Of Western wisdom "surpasses / All the books of the East"'(1994 [1981], p. 65). Herein lies the faultline of what Seth describes as the 'separateness' and 'fear' (1994 [1981], p. 65) attached to the self-conscious acquisition of English. To speak in the desired way is, from now on, to also learn how to speak against oneself. It is to concede, as Seth does toward the end of this poem, that his 'tongue is warped' (1994 [1981], p. 68).

13

To make theoretical sense of Seth's literary illustration of the colonised's complicity in the colonial condition, we need to allow for a more complex understanding of the mechanisms of power. While the logic of power, as critics like Benita Parry insist, is fundamentally coercive, its campaign is frequently seductive. We could say that power traverses the imponderable chasm between coercion and seduction through a variety of baffling self-representations. While it may manifest itself in a show and application of force, it is equally likely to appear as the disinterested purveyor of cultural enlightenment and reform. Through this double representation, power offers itself both as a political limit and as a cultural possibility. If power is at once the qualitative difference or gap between those who have it and those who must suffer it, it also designates an imaginative space that can be occupied, a cultural model that might be imitated and replicated. The apparent political exclusivity of power is thus matched, as Foucault argues, by its web-like inclusiveness:

> Power is employed and exercised through a net-like organisation. And not only do individuals circulate between its threads; they are always in the position of simultaneously undergoing or exercising this power. They are not only its inert or consenting target; they are also the elements of its articulation. In other words, individuals are like vehicles of power, not its points of application (Foucault 1980a, p. 98).

At an obvious level, Foucault's analysis seems to convey the quite basic idea that power is best able to disseminate itself through the collaboration of its subjects. But Foucault's more subtle point is that such apparent 'collaboration' is really symptomatic of the pervasive and claustrophobic omnipresence of power. It is the unavoidable response to a condition where power begins to insinuate itself both inside and outside the world of its victims. Thus, if power is available as a form of 'subjection', it is also a procedure which is 'subjectivised' through, and within, particular individuals. According to Foucault, there is no 'outside' to power—it is always, already, everywhere.

14

In his book *The Intimate Enemy* (1983), Ashis Nandy adapts Foucault's analysis of power to account for the particularly deleterious consequences of the colonial encounter. For Nandy, however, modern colonialism is not just a historical illustration of Foucault's paradigmatic analysis. It is, more significantly, a sort of crucial historical juncture at which power changes its style and first begins to elaborate the strategies of profusion which Foucault theorises so persuasively.

Nandy's book builds on an interesting, if somewhat contentious, distinction between two chronologically distinct types or genres of colonialism. The first, he argues, was relatively simple-minded in its focus on the physical conquest of territories, whereas the second was more insidious in its commitment to the conquest and occupation of minds, selves, cultures. If the first bandit-mode of colonialism was more violent, it was also, as Nandy insists, transparent in its self-interest, greed and rapacity. By contrast, and somewhat more confusingly, the second was pioneered by rationalists, modernists and liberals who argued that imperialism was really the messianic harbinger of civilisation to the uncivilised world.

Despite Nandy's compartmentalisation of militaristic and civilisational imperialism, modern colonialism did, of course, rely on the institutional uses of force and coercion. In addition, it enacted another kind of violence by instituting 'enduring hierarchies of subjects and knowledges—the coloniser and the colonised, the Occidental and the Oriental, the civilised and the primitive, the scientific and the superstitious, the developed and the developing' (Prakash 1995, p. 3). The effect of this schematic reinscription of the colonial relationship is now well acknowledged. The colonised was henceforth to be postulated as the inverse or negative image of the coloniser. In order for Europe to emerge as the site of civilisational plenitude, the colonised world had to be emptied of meaning. Thus, as Nandy writes:

Nandy's notion

This colonialism colonises minds in addition to bodies and it releases forces within colonised societies to alter their cultural priorities once and for all. In the process, it helps to generalise the concept of the modern West from a geographical and temporal entity to a psychological category. The West is now everywhere, within the West and outside, in structures and in minds (Nandy 1983, p. xi).

Colonialism, then, to put it simply, marks the historical process whereby the 'West' attempts systematically to cancel or negate the cultural difference and value of the 'non-West'.

Nandy's psychoanalytic reading of the colonial encounter evokes Hegel's paradigm of the master–slave relationship, and he is not alone in this implicit theoretical debt to Hegel. In fact, whenever postcolonial theory queries what Irene Gendzier describes as 'the Other—directed nature of the reactions of the colonised and his need to struggle to free himself of this externally determined definition of Self' (Gendzier 1973, p. 23), it evokes categories which are reminiscent of Hegel's paradigms.

Hegel's brief but influential notes on 'Lordship and Bondage' are framed by the theorem that human beings acquire identity or self-consciousness only through the recognition of others (see Hegel 1910, vol. 1, pp. 175–88). Each Self has before it another Self in and through which it secures its identity. Initially, there is an antagonism and enmity between these two confronting selves; each aims at the cancellation or death and destruction of the Other. Hence, and temporarily, a situation arises where one is merely recognised while the other recognises. However, the proper end of history—viz. the complete and final revelation of historical truth—requires that the principle of recognition be both mutual and universal. Charles Taylor captures Hegel's conclusions in the following aphorism: 'for what I am, is recognition of man as such and therefore something that in principle should be extended to all' (Taylor 1975, p. 153). As harsh realities would have it, though, it doesn't quite work out this way. The peculiarly human history of servitude, or the historical subordination of one self to another, belies the Hegelian expectation of mutuality.

In his philosophical elaboration of the 'master–slave relationship', Hegel maintains that the master and slave are, initially, locked in a compulsive struggle-unto-death. This goes on until the weak-willed slave, preferring life to liberty, accepts his subjection to the victorious master. When these two antagonists finally face each other after battle, only the master is recognisable. The slave, on the other hand, is now a dependent 'thing' whose existence is shaped by, and as, the conquering Other. Or, as Sartre writes of the slave in his monumental reworking of Hegel's summary text: 'I am possessed by the Other; the Other's look fashions my body in its nakedness, causes it to be born, sculptures it, produces it as it is, sees it as I shall never see it. The Other holds a secret—the secret of what I am' (Sartre 1969; cited in Gendzier 1973, p. 31).

The postcolonial recovery of the colonial condition, which we have been discussing, is, in the first place, an attempt to reveal the coloniser and the colonised as a historical incarnation of Hegel's master and slave. But the task of postcolonial theoretical retrieval cannot stop there. For if history is the record of failure, it also bears testimony to the slave's refusal to concede the master's existential priority. As Nandy tells us, it is crucial for postcolonial theory to take seriously the idea of a psychological resistance to colonialism's civilising mission. To this end, it needs historically to exhume those defences of mind which helped to turn the West 'into a reasonably manageable vector' (Nandy 1983, p. xiii). In this regard it is worth recalling that the slave figure in Sartre's *Being and Nothingness* also makes the following revolutionary pronouncement: 'I lay claim to this being which I am; that is, I wish to recover it, or, more exactly, I am the project of the recovery of my being' (cited in Gendzier 1973, p. 31).

Gandhi and Fanon: the slave's recovery

Colonialism does not end with the end of colonial occupation. However, the psychological resistance to colonialism begins with the onset of colonialism. Thus, the very notion of a 'colonial aftermath' acquires a doubleness, inclusive of both the historical scene of the colonial encounter and its dispersal, in David Lloyd's words, 'among the episodes and fragments of a history still in process' (Lloyd 1993b, p. 11). We have already considered the implications of a theoretical alignment between the adverse symptoms of the 'colonial past' and the 'postcolonial present'. It is also necessary, as Gyan Prakash writes, 'to fully recognise another history of agency and knowledge alive in the dead weight of the colonial past' (Prakash 1995, p. 5). The task of this 'full recognition' requires that acts of anti-colonial resistance be treated not only as theorisable but, as Prakash would have it, as fully comprehensive, fully conceptualised 'theoretical events' in their own right. Thus, Prakash insists, we might start to ascertain the first elaborations of a postcolonial theory itself in historical figures like Gandhi and Frantz Fanon, the anti-colonial Algerian revolutionary. In so doing, we might be guided by Benita Parry's warning against 'the tendency to disown work done within radical traditions other than the most recently enunciated heterodoxies, as necessarily less subversive of the established order' (Parry 1987, p. 27).

Prakash's brilliant juxtaposition of Gandhi and Fanon invites further attention, for in these two figures we find two radically different and yet closely aligned elaborations of postcolonial self-recovery. The differences between Gandhi and Fanon are stark and self-evident. If Gandhi speaks in an anachronistic religio-political vocabulary, Fanon's idiom is shot through with Sartre's existential humanism. If Gandhi's encounter with British imperialism generates a theology of non-violence, Fanon's experience of French colonialism produces a doctrinaire commitment to the redemptive value of collective violence. And if Gandhi enters Indian national politics in middle age, the more impetuous Fanon is dead, after a career of anti-colonial resistance, at the age of 36.

Yet, there are significant similarities between these two revolutionary thinkers. Both of them complete their education in the colonising country—Gandhi to become a reluctant lawyer and Fanon a despairing psychiatrist—and both prepare the theoretical underpinnings of their anti-colonialism in a third country, Gandhi in South Africa and Fanon, despite his

Martiniquian roots, in Algeria. It is probably for this reason that neither Fanon's nor Gandhi's resistance to colonialism is matched by a corresponding nationalism. Both remain wary of the national elite and eventually seek, although equally unsuccessfully, the disbanding of nationalist parties in favour of a more decentralised polity closer to the needs and aspirations of the vast and unacknowledged mass of the Indian and Algerian peasantry. In addition to these theoretical contiguities, Gandhi and Fanon are united in their proposal of a radical style of total resistance to the totalising political and cultural offensive of the colonial civilising mission. To this end, both men carefully elaborate Nandy's notion of a psychological resistance to colonialism. As Fanon wrote toward the end of his revolutionary manifesto in *The Wretched of the Earth*: 'Total liberation is that which concerns all sectors of the personality' (Fanon 1990, p. 250).

The principle underlying Fanon's project of 'total liberation' requires the enslaved figure of the colonised to refuse the privilege of recognition to the colonial 'master'. In Fanon's words: 'Colonialism wants everything to come from it. But the dominant psychological feature of the colonised is to withdraw before any invitation of the conqueror's' (Fanon 1965, p. 63). Fanon's image of a resolute colonised subject politely declining the primacy of Europe appears as the figurative masthead to Gandhi's *Hind Swaraj*—a polemical critique of Western civilisation written in 1909. Whereas Fanon is optimistic and confident about the colonised's ability to valiantly resist the cultural viscosity of Europe, Gandhi's prickly text laments the Indian *moha*, or desire for the superficial glitter of 'modern' civilisation. In his words: 'We brought the English, and we keep them. Why do you forget that our adoption of their civilisation makes their presence in India at all possible? Your hatred against them ought to be transferred to their civilisation' (Gandhi 1938, p. 66).

In their categorical disavowal of cultural colonialism, both thinkers attempt, albeit through very different strategies, to transform anti-colonial dissent into a struggle for creative autonomy from Europe. And it is this quite specific emphasis

19

on creativity rather than authenticity which ultimately prevents both from espousing a nostalgic and uncritical return to the 'pre-colonial' past. Fanon's *The Wretched of the Earth* resounds with an unequivocal 'no' to the 'question of a return to nature' (Fanon 1990, p. 253). So also Gandhi's interrogation of the West is matched by a series of quite heterodox—even heretical—revisions of religious and social tradition. Both thinkers are shaped by an obsession with the rhetoric of futurity. Fanon's revolutionary narrative moves with a compelling urgency toward the recognition that 'the real *leap* consists in introducing invention into existence' (Fanon 1967, p. 229). We might also recall that Gandhi treats his anti-colonial interventions as scientific 'experiments', geared toward the discovery of a hitherto unprecedented political style. While fully acknowledging the complicity or infection of the colonised subject, both men treat the project of national liberation as an imaginative pretext for cultural self-differentiation from Europe and, thereby, as an attempt to exceed, surpass—even improve upon—the claims of Western civilisation. As Fanon writes in his address to the colonised world: 'Let us try to create the whole man, whom Europe has been incapable of bringing to triumphant birth' (Fanon 1990, p. 252). This defiant invitation to alterity or 'civilisational difference' carries within it an accompanying refusal to admit the deficiency or lack which is, as we have seen, the historical predicament of those who have been rendered into slaves.

Fanon's *Black Skin, White Masks* invokes both Hegel and Sartre to diagnose the condition of the colonised slave as a symptom of 'imitativeness'. In Hegel's paradigm, the slave must ultimately turn away from the master to forge the meaning of his existence in labour. He can only regain his integrity by working over the density of matter to which he is henceforth confined. However, as Fanon argues, the racialisation of the master–slave relationship breeds a new and disabling discontent. For whenever the black slave faces the white master, s/he now experiences the disruptive charge of envy and desire. The Negro, Fanon writes, 'wants to be like the master. Therefore he is less independent than the Hegelian slave. In Hegel the slave turns away from the master and turns toward the object. Here the slave turns toward the master and abandons the object' (Fanon 1967, p. 221 note). As both Fanon and Gandhi were to recognise, the slave's hypnotised gaze upon the master condemned this figure to a derivative existence. Herein lay the creative failure of a less than total liberation. In Gandhi's extravagant prose, the problem was this: 'that we want the English rule without the Englishman. You want the tiger's nature but not the tiger . . .' (Gandhi 1938, p. 30). The only way forward, accordingly, was to render the tiger undesirable.

Gandhi's and Fanon's powerful attempt to demystify the claims of Western civic society forces the allegorical figure of the slave to consider its own history as the terrible consequence of the master's privileges. Rather than see itself *as*, or in the image of, the master, the slave is now urged to see itself *beside* the master. It is compelled, to borrow Homi Bhabha's words, to envision 'the image of post-Enlightenment man tethered to, not confronted by, his dark reflection, the shadow of colonised man, that splits his presence, distorts his outline, breaches his boundaries . . . disturbs and distorts the very time of his being' (Bhabha 1994, p. 44). It is with this agenda in mind, that Gandhi and Fanon rewrite the narrative of Western modernity to include the repressed and marginalised figures of its victims. In this revised version, industrialisation tells the story of economic exploitation, democracy is splintered by the protesting voices of the suffragettes, technology combines with warfare, and the history of medicine is attached relentlessly by Fanon to the techniques of torture. If Gandhi's *Hind Swaraj* everywhere discerns the structural violence of Western 'modernity', Fanon is equally unsparing in his denunciation of the European myths of progress and humanism: 'When I search for Man in the technique and the style of Europe, I see only a succession of negations of man, and an avalanche of murders' (Fanon 1990, p. 252). Read together, the Gandhian and Fanonian critiques of Western civilisation sketch the ethical inadequacy and undesirability of the colonial 'master' whose cognition, as Nandy writes, 'has to exclude the slave except as a "thing"' (Nandy 1983, p. xvi). There is no space for

21

desire, as Fanon and Gandhi struggle to convey, in the existential limitations of a condition whose 'humanity' is founded on the inhumane pathology of racism and violence.

We know, of course, that the operations of desire are rarely informed by the reflections of judgment; Seth's poet-narrator in 'Diwali' desires Western knowledge despite his knowledge of Western imperialism. In a sense, it is irrelevant to ask whether Gandhi and Fanon successfully cured the colonised world of its perverse and self-defeating longing for the conqueror. Nor must we feel compelled to condone their fierce and uncompromising rejection of all things European. Nevertheless, the careful retrieval of figures like Gandhi and Fanon is instructive to postcolonial theory. For when this theory returns to the colonial scene, it finds two stories: the seductive narrative of power, and alongside that the counter-narrative of the colonised—politely, but firmly, declining the come-on of colonialism. It is important to re-member both—to remember, in other words, that postcoloniality derives its genealogy from both narratives. We might conclude this introduction by remembering a possibly apocryphal story about Gandhi. Journalistic legend has it that once, when in England, Gandhi was asked the following question by an earnest young reporter: 'Mr Gandhi, what do you think of modern civilisation?'. In some versions of the story Gandhi laughed heartily, in others, became very serious, before replying: 'I think it would be a very good idea'.

2

Thinking otherwise: a brief intellectual history

Having sketched out the over-arching preoccupations and obligations of postcolonial studies, we might now turn our attention to the intellectual history of this new discipline. Although postcolonial theory has been instrumental, over the last fifteen years or so, in bringing a new prominence to matters of colony and empire, it is by no means unique or inaugural in its academic concern with the subject of imperialism. So too it is methodologically and conceptually indebted to a variety of both earlier and more recent 'Western' theories. The purpose of this chapter is to situate postcolonialism within a contemporary and metropolitan theoretical landscape, and to indicate some of its theoretical influences and points of departure.

Marxism, poststructuralism and the problem of humanism

In the excitement over what appears to be a 'new' focus on colonial issues, students of postcolonialism tend to ignore (or forget) the long history of specifically Marxist anti-imperialist thought. Ever since the first decade of this century, Marxist thinkers—such as Lenin, Bukharin and Hilferding, to name a few—have been urging the Western world to concede that the story of colonialism is a necessary sub-plot to the emergence of market society in Europe, and to the concomitant globalisation of capital (see Brewer 1980; Hobsbawm 1987; Warren 1980). And yet, despite the rigorous and wide-ranging work conducted under its aegis, the Marxist engagement with imperialism has secured only a very limited constituency. Few critics have continued an exclusively Marxist interrogation of empire, and those who have, are vehemently opposed to the prevailing postcolonialist orthodoxy. Aijaz Ahmad, for example, has been especially vociferous in his insistence upon the theoretical and political incompatibility between Marxist and postcolonialist positions. As he writes: 'we should speak not so much of colonialism or postcolonialism but of capitalist modernity, which takes the colonial form in particular places and at particular times' (Ahmad 1995, p. 7). Postcolonial analysis, in turn, rarely acknowledges a genealogical debt to its Marxist predecessors—in fact, its engagement with Marxist theory is often explicitly antagonistic. In this it is guided, albeit mistakenly, by the assumption that Marxism has failed to direct a comprehensive critique against colonial history and ideology.

Jameson is instructive in his account of the postcolonialist bias against Marxism:

> The very widely held contemporary belief—that, following the title of Walter Rodney's influential book, capitalism leads . . . to 'the development of underdevelopment', and that imperialism systematically cripples the growth of its colonies and its dependent areas—this belief is utterly absent from the first moment of Marxist theories of imperialism and is indeed everywhere contradicted by them, where they raise the matter at all (Jameson 1990, p. 47).

For reasons of its own very specific reading of the developments of capitalism in the late nineteenth century, Marxism has been unable to theorise colonialism as an exploitative relationship between the West and its Others. Accordingly—as Jameson concedes—it has also neglected to address sympathetically the historical, cultural and political alterity, or difference, of the colonised world and, in so doing, it has relinquished its potential appeal to postcolonialist thought. Where, then, does postcolonialism begin? Where, in other words, does it seek its appropriate intellectual inheritance?

While the publication of Said's *Orientalism* in 1978 is commonly regarded as the principal catalyst and reference point for postcolonial theory, insufficient attention is given to the fact that this ur-text (and its followers) evolved within a distinctly poststructuralist climate, dominated in the Anglo-American academy by the figures of Foucault and Derrida. Indeed, Said's own work draws upon a variety of Foucauldian paradigms. In particular, Foucault's notion of a discourse, as elaborated in *The Archaeology of Knowledge* and in *Discipline and Punish,* informs Said's attempt to isolate the principle and workings of Orientalism. In addition, Gayatri Spivak first gained admission to the literary-critical pantheon through her celebrated translation of Derrida's *Of Grammatology* in 1977. And much of her subsequent work has been preoccupied with the task of dialogue and negotiation with and between Derrida and Foucault. Arguably, then, it is through poststucturalism and postmodernism—and their deeply fraught and ambivalent relationship with Marxism—that postcolonialism starts to distil its particular provenance.

Some hostile critics have been quick to attribute the links between postcolonialism and poststructuralism to temporal contingency and, therefore, to academic fashion alone. And in truth the alliance with poststructuralism has indeed enabled postcolonialism to gain a privileged foothold within the metropolitan academic mainstream. Poststructuralist thought has, for example, provided a somewhat more substantial impetus to the postcolonial studies project through its clear and confidently theorised proposal for a Western critique of Western civilisation. In pursuing the terms of this critique, postcolonialism has also inherited a very specific understanding of Western domination as the symptom of an unwholesome alliance between power and knowledge. Thus, in a shift from the predominantly economic paradigms of Marxist thought, postcolonialism has learnt—through its poststructuralist parentage—to diagnose the material effects and implications of colonialism as an epistemological malaise at the heart of Western rationality. It has also learnt to be suspicious of 'the problem of universalism/Eurocentrism that was inherent in Marxist (or for that matter liberal) thought itself' (Chakrabarty 1993, p. 422). According to Dipesh Chakrabarty, it was the recognition of this problem which led the postcolonialist historians engaged in the Subaltern Studies collective to be 'receptive to the critiques of marxist historicism—in particular to the "incredulity toward grand narratives"—that French post-structuralist thinkers popularised in the English-language world in the 1980s' (1993, p. 422).

For all its pondering on questions of 'difference', however, Derrida's and Foucault's work does not really address the problem of colonialism directly. It is only in an early essay, 'George Canguilhem: philosopher of error', that Foucault explicitly equates European knowledges and the mirage of Western rationality with the 'economic domination and political hegemony' of colonialism (Foucault 1980b, p. 54). Similarly, Derrida's 'White mythology: metaphor in the text of philosophy', (Derrida 1974) stands out for its suggestion that the very structure of Western rationality is racist and imperialist. Both essays are, however, typical of Derrida's and Foucault's oeuvre in their unhesitating challenge to the universal validity of Western culture and epistemology, and it is in this challenge, as Spivak tells us, that postcolonialist thought secures its desired intellectual moorings:

> Where I was first brought up—when I first read Derrida I didn't know who he was, I was very interested to see that he was actually dismantling the philosophical tradition from *inside* rather than from *outside*, because of course we were brought up in an education system in India where the name of the hero of that philosophical system was the universal human being, and we were taught that if we could begin to approach an internationalisation of that human being, then we could be human. When I saw in France someone was actually trying to dismantle the tradition which told us what

would make us human, that seemed rather interesting too (Spivak 1990, p. 7).

What is the tradition that Spivak is speaking of here? How is it dismantled through the poststructuralist intervention? And how does the liberated understanding of what it means to be a human being reflect upon the postcolonial studies project? We might begin to address some of these questions by stopping to examine the shibboleth of Western 'humanism'—which is also the name that Derrida and Foucault give to the tradition they seek to dismantle.

'Humanism' is a highly contentious term. As Bernauer and Mahon point out, for example, 'Christianity, the critique of Christianity, science, anti-science, Marxism, existentialism, personalism, National Socialism, and Stalinism have each won the label "humanism" for a time' (Bernauer & Mahon 1994, pp. 141–2). These various humanisms are, however, unified in their belief that underlying the diversity of human experience it is possible, first, to discern a universal and given human nature, and secondly to find it revealed in the common language of rationality. In defence of this belief, Marxist exponents of humanistic principles, such as Noam Chomsky, Fredric Jameson and Jurgen Habermas have argued that humanism holds out the possibility of a rational and universal consensus between responsible individuals with regard to the conceptualisation of a humane, progressive and just social order. In contrast, poststructuralist and postmodernist anti-humanists maintain that any universal or normative postulation of rational unanimity is totalitarian and hostile to the challenges of otherness and difference.

For these critics, the very ideas of 'rationality' and 'human nature' are historical constructions and therefore subject to historical investments and limitations. This view is self-evidently appealing to the postcolonial concern with cultural diversity. At the same time, and somewhat painfully for postcolonial studies, the debate between Marxist humanists and poststructuralist anti-humanists remains unresolved on the subject of ethics and politics. Political mobilisation and ethical

27

principles, as Marxist critics forcefully argue, necessarily require some sort of cross-cultural consensus. For a postmodern thinker like Lyotard, however, the very process of reaching consensus is vitiated by a 'conversational imperialism'. According to Lyotard, the participants in an ethico-political dialogue are rarely equal, and almost never equally represented in the final consensus. Insofar as this dialogue is already projected towards some predetermined end—such as justice or rationality—it is always conducted, as Dipesh Chakrabarty argues, 'within a field of possibilities that is already structured from the very beginning in favour of certain outcomes' (Chakrabarty 1995, p. 757). One of the participants invariably 'knows better' than the other, whose world view, in turn, must be modified or 'improved' in the reaching of consensus. The heterogeneity of thought, Lyotard would argue, can only ever be preserved through the refusal of unanimity and the search for a radical 'discensus'. Thus, and we will return to this problem in subsequent chapters, postcolonial studies critics are left to ponder the apparent chasm between the poststructuralist insistence on the impossibility of a universal human nature and the opposing Marxist verdict on the impossibility of a politics which lacks the principle of 'solidarity'.

In understanding postcolonialism's vexed relationship with humanism, it is important to recognise that postcolonial studies inherits two chronologically distinct, if ideologically overlapping, approaches to the history and consequences of humanism. The first is concerned with humanism as a cultural and educational program which began in Renaissance Italy in about the mid-sixteenth century and evolved progressively into the area of studies we now practise and preach as the humanities. The second distinctly poststructuralist approach brings a more precise meaning and imprecise chronology to bear upon the notion of humanism. It identifies humanism with the theory of subjectivity and knowledge philosophically inaugurated by Bacon, Descartes and Locke, and scientifically substantiated by Galileo and Newton. This philosophical and scientific revolution is said to find its proper fulfilment in the eighteenth century, where it comes to be embraced as the Enlightenment or *Aufklärung.*

There are vast differences between the literary humanism of sixteenth-century Florence and the scientific humanism of eighteenth-century Europe. Nevertheless, both types of humanism are unanimous in their anthropocentricism or categorical valorisation of the human subject. Man, as Diderot observes in the mood of his Renaissance predecessor Petrarch, 'is the single place from which we must begin and to which we must refer everything . . . It is the presence of man which makes the existence of beings meaningful' (cited in Gay 1977, p. 162). Correspondingly, the status of human-ness is intimately bound up with questions of knowledge. Both thinkers presuppose a symbiotic and reciprocal relationship between what man is (and I use 'man' advisedly) and what man knows—with one crucial difference of emphasis. Renaissance humanism and its inheritors insist that man is made human by the things he knows, that is, by the curricular *content* of his knowledge and education. Accordingly, it is predominantly concerned with the role and function of pedagogy. In contrast, Enlightenment humanism and its legatees take 'humanity' to be a function of the *way* in which man knows things. Its concern, accordingly, is with the structure of epistemology or the basis and validity of knowledge. The Enlightenment, as Charles Taylor writes, generates 'an epistemological revolution with anthropological consequences' (Taylor 1975, p. 5). It changes the way in which we have come to know the notion of Self. It furnishes, in other words, the modern understanding of subjectivity.

While both of the humanisms we have been discussing assert that all human beings are, as it were, the measure of all things, they simultaneously smuggle a disclaimer into their celebratory outlook. The humanist valorisation of man is almost always accompanied by a barely discernible corollary which suggests that some human beings are more human than others—either on account of their access to superior learning, or on account of their cognitive faculties. The historical logic of these humanist subclauses is illustrated in Thomas

Babington Macaulay's infamous minute of 1835 regarding the introduction of English education in colonial India:

> The intrinsic superiority of the Western literature is indeed fully admitted by those members of the committee who support the oriental plan of education . . . It is, I believe, no exaggeration to say that all the historical information which has been collected in the Sanskrit language is less valuable than what may be found in the paltry abridgments used at preparatory schools in England (cited in Said 1983, p. 12).

Writing in a similar vein, the Reverend J. Tucker attributes India's civilisational inferiority to the pathological deficiency of the native mind, namely, to the 'dulness [sic] of their comprehension' (cited in Viswanathan 1989, p. 6). Reading backward from this nineteenth-century debate on colonial education, we might say that the underside of Western humanism produces the dictum that since some human beings are more human than others, they are more substantially the measure of all things. With this in mind, we can begin to direct a poststructuralist gaze upon Diderot's contemporaries and forefathers.

What is Enlightenment?

In November 1784, the liberal German periodical *Berlinische Monatschrift* published a response to the question 'Was ist Aufklärung', that is, 'What is Enlightenment?'. The respondent was none other than the philosopher Immanuel Kant, considered by many to represent the high point of Enlightenment rationality. In this brief and occasional essay—by no means a major piece of work—Kant argues that the Enlightenment offers mankind a way out of, or exit from, immaturity into the improved condition of maturity. The Enlightenment, he maintains, is the possibility whereby man philosophically acquires the status and capacities of a rational and adult being.

Some two centuries after the publication of Kant's confident response, Foucault revisits the scene of the 1784 *Berlinische Monatschrift* to reiterate the question: 'What is Enlightenment?'. By resuscitating this question, Foucault strategically suggests that Kant's initial response and, indeed, the very project of Enlightenment rationality, is far from conclusive. The historical event of the Enlightenment, he argues, 'did not make us mature adults . . . we have not reached that stage yet' (Foucault 1984a, p. 49). In making this statement, Foucault is not so much mourning our collective failure to become adults, as gesturing toward our philosophical and ethical obligation to exceed the limits of Kantian maturity, or what he calls the 'blackmail' of the Enlightenment. If Kantian philosophy instructs us to be, know, do, and hope in universal ways, Foucault's response is to interrogate and historicise 'the contingency that has made us what we are'. It is only through this process that we might liberate the alterity and diversity of human existence or, in his words, discover 'the possibility of no longer being, doing or thinking what we are, do or think' (Foucault 1984a, p. 46). To this end, Foucault asks many questions of Kant and the history of Enlightenment rationality. One such question, especially meaningful for postcolonial purposes, focuses on Kant's suggestion that the Enlightenment holds out the possibility of 'maturity' for all humanity, for 'mankind' at large:

> A . . . difficulty appears here in Kant's text, in his use of the word 'mankind', *Menschheit*. The importance of this word in the Kantian conception of history is well known. Are we to understand that the entire human race is caught up in the process of Enlightenment? In that case, we must imagine Enlightenment as a historical change that affects the political and social existence of all people on the face of the earth. *Or are we to understand that it involves a change affecting what constitutes the humanity of human beings?* (my emphasis; Foucault 1984a, p. 35)

Through his seemingly open-ended interrogation, Foucault establishes that the Kantian conception of 'mankind' is prescriptive rather than descriptive. Instead of reflecting the radical heterogeneity of human nature, it restricts the ostensibly universal structures of human existence to the normative

31

condition of adult rationality—itself a value arising from the specific historicity of European societies. It follows that this account of 'humanity' precludes the possibility of dialogue with other ways of being human and, in fact, brings into existence and circulation the notion of the 'non-adult' as 'inhuman'. Needless to say, this move also instantiates and sets into motion a characteristically pedagogic and imperialist hierarchy between European adulthood and its childish, colonised Other.

Postcolonial theory recognises that colonial discourse typically rationalises itself through rigid oppositions such as maturity/immaturity, civilisation/barbarism, developed/developing, progressive/primitive. Critics like Ashis Nandy have especially drawn attention to the colonial use of the homology between childhood and the state of being colonised. In this regard, V. G. Kiernan's observations about the African experience of colonialism are generally revealing:

> The notion of the African as minor . . . took very strong hold. Spaniards and Boers had questioned whether natives had souls: modern Europeans cared less about that but doubted whether they had minds, or minds capable of adult growth. A theory came to be fashionable that mental growth in the African ceased early, that childhood was never left behind (cited in Nandy 1983, p. 15 note).

This perception of the colonised culture as fundamentally childlike or childish feeds into the logic of the colonial 'civilising mission' which is fashioned, quite self-consciously, as a form of tutelage or a disinterested project concerned with bringing the colonised to maturity. Macaulay's interventions into the proper education of colonised Indians, for instance, are informed by the sense that colonialism is really a 'developmental' project. The coloniser, in his understanding, is principally, if not exclusively, an educator:

> What is power worth if it is founded on vice, on ignorance, and on misery; if we can hold it only by violating the most sacred duties which as governors we owe to the governed and which, as a people blessed with far more than ordinary

measure of political liberty and of intellectual light, we owe to a race debased by three thousand years of despotism and priestcraft. We are free, we are civilised to little purpose, if we grudge to any portion of the human race an equal measure of freedom and civilisation (cited in Viswanathan 1989, pp. 16–17).

Macaulay's defence of the pedagogical motivations of colonialism betrays its Enlightenment legacy, namely, the sense that European rationality holds out the possibility of improvement for all of humanity. Accordingly, those who are already in possession of the gospel of rationality are seen to have an ethical obligation or 'calling' to spread the word and proselytise on behalf of their emancipatory creed. Civilised minds, as Christoph Martin Wieland wrote, are bound to 'do the great work to which we have been called: to cultivate, enlighten and ennoble the human race' (cited in Gay 1977, p. 13).

The Enlightenment expositions of Kant, Wieland and Macaulay have gained several followers and sustained many revisionary accounts of colonialism. For Marx, somewhat notoriously, the benefits of British colonialism more than compensated for its violence and injustices. 'Whatever may have been the crimes of England', he argues, 'she was the unconscious tool of history', which raised India—in this instance—from its semi-barbaric state into the improved condition of modernity (cited in Said 1991, p. 153). Against the coercive logic of these arguments, we may recall that for Lyotard, 'immaturity' is not so much the failure of modernity as the possibility of a truly humane philosophy. If the Enlightenment seeks its humanism in the decisive and aggressive rationality of adulthood, the task of postmodernity, as Lyotard sees it, is to salvage the tentative philosophical indeterminacy of childhood:

> Shorn of speech, incapable of standing upright, hesitating over the objects of its interest, not able to calculate its advantages, not sensitive to common reason, the child is eminently the human because its distress heralds and promises things possible. Its initial delay in humanity, which makes it the hostage of the adult community, is also what manifests to this

community the lack of humanity it is suffering from, and which calls on it to become more human (Lyotard 1991, pp. 3–4).

Rather than dismissing Lyotard's account of childhood as foolishly romantic or essentialising, it is crucial to recognise it as a rhetorical response to the Kantian policing of human nature. Seen from a postcolonial studies perspective, his disruption of the boundaries between the human and the inhuman helps to undo the logic of the colonial civilising mission—as Spivak would have it—*from inside* the Western philosophical tradition.

Descartes' error

The journey between Kantian adulthood and postmodern childhood, that is, between the Enlightenment and its critics, has its basis in an earlier history which officially begins in late November 1619. This is the birth date of Cartesian philosophy, recorded by Descartes himself at the beginning of his *Olympica*: 'On the tenth of November 1619 . . . I was full of enthusiasm and finding the foundations of a marvelous science . . .' (cited in Gilson 1963, p. 57). Descartes' discovery arguably spawns the Enlightenment philosophy, which Kant confidently defends in the *Berlinische Monatschrift*. So also the poststructuralist/postmodern critique of Western civilisation properly begins with a counter-assessment of Cartesianism.

The date 10 November 1619 marks the decisive and systematic advent of anti-agnostic, secularism in Western philosophy. It marks Descartes' attempt to enthrone man at the centre of epistemology and, simultaneously, to make knowledge impregnable to doubt. We might say that this date confirms humanism as the basis for certain knowledge, or conversely, as Sartre puts it, 'the Cartesian *cogito* becomes the only possible *point de départ* for existentialism and the only possible basis for humanism' (Sartre 1946, p. 191). Generally speaking, Cartesian philosophy produces three revolutionary variants on the notion of the Self and its relationship to

34

knowledge and thereby to the external world. These are the notions of the self-defining subject of consciousness; the all-knowing subject of consciousness; and, finally, the formally empowered subject of consciousness. To clarify our understanding of this self-centred philosophy, we might look at the methodical process through which each of these notions is delivered.

Descartes introduces the self-defining subject of consciousness or the self-affirming ego through a simple inquiry into the things we know for certain. His meditations on this subject eventually lead to the troubling conclusion that there is nothing we know that is entirely beyond doubt—with one notable exception. Even though we may doubt the existence of the world and of external reality, we know, Descartes argues, that we exist. We know this even in the painful acuity of doubt as the very capacity to doubt gestures toward the activity of thought which, in turn, presupposes the fact of existence or self-consciousness. If I think, therefore, I am. Paradoxically, the certainty of my existence is established in the very uncertainty of my doubt. Seen in this way, the Cartesian *cogito*, or the 'I think' of his famous conclusion, makes, as Bertrand Russell puts it, 'mind more certain than matter, and my mind more certain than the minds of others' (Russell 1961, p. 548). In all philosophy which descends from Descartes it follows that matter is only knowable 'by inference of what is known of mind' (Russell 1961, p. 548). The crux of this philosophy is, in other words, the all-knowing subject of consciousness—an entity which insists that our knowledge of the world is nothing other than the narcissism of self-consciousness. At this turn in Cartesian philosophy, when the world is rendered into a giant mirror, man enters the scene of Western knowledge as, in Foucault's words, 'an emperico-transcendental doublet'. He is postulated as 'a being such that knowledge will be attained in him of what renders all knowledge possible' (Foucault 1970, p. 318).

The Cartesian celebration of the human subject's epistemological possibilities is inevitably accompanied by an assertion of its power over, and freedom from, the external world of objects.

This power—founded in knowledge—recognises that nature is threatening only, and insofar as, it is mysterious and incalculable. In response to this threat, the elaborations of *cogito* reduce the unintelligible diversity and material alterity of the world to the familiar contents of our minds. This opens up the possibility of ordering or taming the wild profusion of things formally, according to the structure of the subject's emancipatory rationality, and similarly to the terms of a mathematical demonstration. We need to remember here that Descartes privileges mathematics as the cognitive method most favourable to the function of rationality or *ratio*. But, as Weber argued, a mathematical perception of the world is ultimately a 'theft' of its inherent—uncontainable and unquantifiable—value or meaning. The offending thief, in this instance, is the formally empowered subject of consciousness: 'there are no mysterious incalculable forces that come into play, but rather that one can, in principle, master all things by calculation. This means that the world is disenchanted' (Weber 1930, p. 139).

To think of the world mathematically, that is, as *mathesis*, thus requires a reductive application of a few abstract and generalising principles to the multiplicity of particular things. It requires a progression from *theoria*, or theory, to *praxis*, or practice, rather than the other way around. Seen in this way, Cartesian *mathesis* is clearly the basis of the Enlightenment universalism that we earlier encountered in Kant. It is, as Foucault writes, 'an exhaustive ordering of the world as though methods, concepts, types of analysis, and finally men themselves, had all been displaced at the behest of a fundamental network defining the implicit and inevitable unity of knowledge' (Foucault 1970, pp. 75–6). That is to say, it proposes a global and unitary view of thought which maintains that if all things are knowable in the same way, they must be virtually identical. This is the logic which later leads Foucault to claim that 'the history of the order imposed on things would be . . . a history of the Same' (1970, p. xxiv). These 'histories' of universal knowledge and self-identical subjectivity which Foucault speaks of are in turn engineered by the humanist impulse to, as Descartes wrote 'make ourselves masters and possessors of nature' (cited in Gilson 1963, p. 74). They chronicle an equation of power with knowledge which Bacon, much before Foucault, announced with the tag: 'the sovereignty of man lieth hid in knowledge'.

Whose sovereignty? Which men? What history? These are some of the questions that postcolonial studies, along with its poststructuralist allies, asks of Descartes and the Enlightenment. Let us end this section with the *Encyclopaedia Britannica*, which proudly informed its readers in the 1770s that the discoveries and improvements of eighteenth-century inventors 'diffuse a glory over this country unattainable by conquest or domination' (cited in Gay 1977, p. 9). In issuing this statement, the editors of the *Encyclopaedia* do not dissociate knowledge from the violence of 'conquest or domination' so much as announce its even greater capacity for enslavement. Reason is the weapon of Enlightenment philosophy and, accordingly, the problem for anti-Enlightenment thought. Is it possible, after 10 November 1619, to imagine non-coercive knowledges? Is it possible, as Gandhi would have asked, to think non-violently?

Nietzsche's genealogy

The anti-Cartesian turn in Foucault, Derrida and Lyotard, which we have been following, develops out of a long line of thinkers stretching from Max Weber to Martin Heidegger, through to Theodor Adorno and Max Horkheimer. Each of these thinkers is concerned with the destructive powers of Western rationality, and all of them invoke the nihilistic figure of Nietzsche to bolster their onslaught on the epistemological narcissism of Western culture—that is to say, the narcissism released into the world through Descartes' self-defining, all-knowing and formally empowered subject of consciousness.

Nietzsche's paradigmatic critique, as Foucault points out in a significant essay entitled 'Nietzsche, genealogy, history', is directed at two foundational humanist myths: the myth of pure origins and the emancipatory myth of progress and teleology.

37

Foucault postulates Nietzsche's anti-humanism as an excavation at the archaeological site of origins, where it works relentlessly and systematically to reveal a formative deficiency in the historical beginnings of all humanist institutions, ideas and concepts. The Western humanist thinks of the 'origin' as the place of plenitude, presence and truth. The Nietzschian archaeologist, on the other hand, can only find the residual traces of malice, theft, greed and disparity at the start of human history. In other words, s/he discovers that a Fall prefigures and disfigures the purity of Genesis. Seen as such, the very idea of Genesis—of unadulterated origins—is shown as a supplement, or as a mythical compensation for an originary lack. 'We wished', Nietzsche writes, 'to awaken to the feeling of man's sovereignty by showing his divine birth: this faith is now forbidden, since a monkey stands at the entrance' (cited in Foucault 1984b, p. 79).

Nietzsche's 'destructive' endeavour directly foreshadows the method and intent of contemporary deconstructive philosophy which, likewise, scavenges in the forgotten archives of Western humanism to reveal its suppressed inadequacies, ruptures and paradoxes. Thus, for Derrida, as for Nietzsche, the outset of all emancipatory social discourse betrays the shared origins of morality and immorality; it is marked by the 'non-ethical opening of ethics' (cited in Norris 1982, p. 39). So also it is possible to discern an inevitable lack and the persistent naggings of doubt in the confident self-presence and aggressive certitude of Descartes' *cogito*. While the subject who 'thinks', Derrida and Foucault would argue, may not 'know' his own limitations, the uneven history of rationality testifies to the civilisational failure of the Cartesian project—which begins as it ends in violence: reason, as Foucault writes in his gloss on Nietzsche, 'was born . . . from chance; devotion to truth and the precision of scientific methods arose from the passion of scholars, their reciprocal hatred, their fanatical and unending discussions, and their spirit of competition—their personal conflicts that slowly forged the weapons of reason' (Foucault 1984b, p. 78). Accordingly, the vitiated beginnings of rationality fulfil their logic in the progressive deterioration,

Nietzsche is anti-Western humanism

rather than emancipation, of humanity. The atavistic flaw of *cogito* is re-enacted in a perverse evolution from error to cumulative error, from petty to genocidal violence: 'Humanity', in Foucault's somewhat apocalyptic words, 'does not gradually proceed from combat to combat until it arrives at universal reciprocity, where the rule of law finally replaces warfare; humanity installs each of its violences in a system of rules and thus proceeds from domination to domination' (p. 85).

By the time Nietzsche's diatribe on the flawed origins and teleology of Western humanism is fully absorbed into the poststructuralist and postmodernist thematic, it acquires two specific and more clearly articulated objections to the Cartesian theory of epistemological subjectivity—first, to its philosophy of identity, and second to its account of knowledge as a power over objective reality. Both of these objections are especially resonant for postcolonial studies, as they hold out the possibility of theorising a non-coercive relationship or dialogue with the excluded 'Other' of Western humanism.

The first objection is developed through Heidegger, Foucault, Derrida and Lyotard, each of whom maintains that the Cartesian philosophy of identity is premised upon an ethically unsustainable omission of the Other. For Heidegger— seen by many to be the 'archetype and trend-setter of postmodernism' (Bauman 1992, p. ix)—the all-knowing and self-sufficient Cartesian subject violently negates material and historical alterity/Otherness in its narcissistic desire to always see the world in its own self-image. This anthropocentric world view is ultimately deficient on account of its indifference to difference, and consequent refusal to accommodate that which is not human. Thus, as far as Heidegger is concerned, the Cartesian *cogito* fails adequately to think out the 'Being of a stone or even life as the Being of plants and animals' (Heidegger 1977, p. 206). For Foucault, similarly, that which is 'unthought' in *cogito* becomes a synonym for the Other of Western rationality: 'the unthought . . . is not lodged in man like a shrivelled-up nature or a stratified history; it is, in relation to man, the Other' (Foucault 1970, p. 326). While Heidegger seeks the quality of alterity in the natural and non-human world, Foucault substantially extends the notion of Otherness to cover criminality, madness, disease, foreigners, homosexuals, strangers, women. Derrida's name for these excluded Others is the 'remainder', and Lyotard seeks their irreducible presence in the singularity and plurality of what he calls the 'event'.

The poststructuralist/postmodern postulation of the 'unthought', the 'remainder' and the 'event' is crucial for its illustration of the unsustainable discrepancy between the finitude of the thinking rational subject and the infinite variety of the world—which is simply in excess of what 'Western man' can, or does, think. Examined in this way, the presence of the Cartesian subject is simultaneously revealed as the locus of absence, omission, exclusion and silence. This subject is—to come full circle—diagnosed as the source of the epistemological poverty which informs Western humanism. Far from being the reservoir of certain and complete knowledge, Cartesian 'man', as Foucault writes, 'is also the source of misunderstanding—of misunderstanding that constantly exposes his thought to the risk of being swamped by his own being, and also enables him to recover his integrity on the basis of what eludes him' (1970, p. 323).

It is not enough, however, to leave Cartesian man in this state of benign misunderstanding and forgetfulness. In addition to simply omitting the Other, Descartes' philosophy of identity is also sustained through a violent and coercive relationship with its omitted Other. As Zygmunt Bauman writes: 'Since the sovereignty of the modern intellect is the power to define and make definitions stick—everything that eludes unequivocal allocation is an anomaly and a challenge' (Bauman 1991, p. 9). Accordingly, just as modern rationality has often attributed a dangerous Otherness to the figure(s) of the deviant, it has also endeavoured violently to repress all symptoms of cultural alterity. In a contentious move, writers like Adorno, Horkheimer and Bauman have identified fascism as one product of the Enlightenment's fear of alterity. The procedures of the colonial civilising mission are, arguably, motivated by similar anxieties.

Lyotard's observations on the levelling action of Western humanism are instructive here:

> the grand narratives of legitimation which characterise modernity in the West . . . are cosmopolitical, as Kant would say. They involve precisely an 'overcoming' (*dépassement*) of the particular cultural identity in favour of a universal civic identity. But how such an overcoming can take place is not apparent (Lyotard 1992, pp. 44–5).

assimilation

Postcolonial studies, we might say, joins postmodernism in an attempt to analyse and to resist this *dépassement*.

Before concluding this poststructuralist account of Enlightenment humanism, I would like to briefly return to Kant's essay in the *Berlinische Monatschrift*. In the course of this essay, Kant tells his readers that the Enlightenment has a motto: *Aude sapere*, or 'Dare to know'. Herein lies the history of Western humanism and Cartesian rationality. To know with daring is henceforth to be bold, impudent, defiant, audacious in the exercise of knowledge. It is, in other words, to concede mastery as the single motivation for knowing the world. The poststructuralist and postmodern intervention into this field delivers the *possibility* of knowing differently—of knowing difference in and for itself. In sharp contrast with the Enlightenment, its motto could well be 'Care to know'. Let us end with Levinas: 'It is in the laying down by the ego of its sovereignty (in its "hateful" modality) that we find ethics . . .' (Levinas 1994, p. 85).

3

Postcolonialism and the new humanities

In the previous chapter a distinction was made between Western *humanism* and the Western *humanities* on the grounds that while the former is concerned with ways of knowing, or acquiring knowledge, the latter proposes that man is made human by the things he knows. We have already examined the principal features of postcolonialism's inherited deconstructive bias against Enlightenment humanism. This chapter will supply a context for its oppositional stance against the traditional humanities.

Provincialising Europe

Ever since its development in the 1980s, postcolonialism has found itself in the company of disciplines such as women's studies, cultural studies and gay/lesbian studies. These new fields of knowledge—often classified under the rubric of the 'new humanities'—have endeavoured first, to foreground the exclusions and elisions which confirm the privileges and authority of canonical knowledge systems, and second to recover those marginalised knowledges which have been occluded and silenced by the entrenched humanist curriculum.

Each of these disciplinary areas has attempted to represent the interests of a particular set of 'subjugated knowledges', which is Foucault's term for 'knowledges that have been disqualified as inadequate to their task or insufficiently elaborated: naive knowledges, located low down on the hierarchy, beneath the required level of cognition or scienticity' (Foucault 1980a, p. 82). These 'minor' knowledges, as Deleuze and Guattari write, embody forms of thought and culture which have been been violently 'deterritorialised' by major or dominant knowledge systems (Deleuze & Guattari 1986). Foucault's and Deleuze's terminology deliberately invests the struggle over the subject of knowledge with the language of political insurrection. For Foucault, the proposal for a radical reclamation of subjugated/minor knowledges helps to expose the hidden contiguity between knowledge and power, 'through which a society conveys its knowledge and ensures its survival under the mask of knowledge' (Foucault 1977, p. 225). Deleuze, likewise, postulates the 'reterritorialisation' of minor literatures as 'the relay for a revolutionary machine-to-come' (Deleuze & Guattari 1986, p. 18).

A characteristic example of this type of project may be found within feminist/women's studies, which recognises that the disempowerment of women has been facilitated, in part, through their exclusion from the space where knowledge proper is constituted and disseminated. The acquisition of knowledge, as Susan Sheridan points out, has been an integral and established feature of feminist activism since at least the nineteenth century (see Sheridan 1990, p. 40). The feminist movement has consistently demanded equal access to the *means* of knowledge and also equal participation in the *making* of knowledge on the grounds that inherited knowledges are hopelessly constrained by the preoccupations of the predominantly male institutions within which they have been developed and validated. The feminist intervention into the humanities academy has thus posed a challenge to the normative and universalist assumptions of gender-biased or 'phallogocentric' knowledge systems, and attempted, in turn, to make both the ways of knowing and the things known more representative.

Its aim has been to enable women to become the active participating subjects rather than the passive and reified objects of knowledge.

Postcolonial studies follows feminism in its critique of seemingly foundational discourses. Unlike feminism, however, it directs its critique against the cultural hegemony of European knowledges in an attempt to reassert the epistemological value and agency of the non-European world. The postcolonial reclamation of non-European knowledges is, in effect, a refutation of Macaulay's infamous privileging of a single shelf of a 'good' European library over the entire corpus of 'Oriental' literary production. Macaulay's 1835 minute typifies the historical colonisation of scholarship and pedagogy whereby, as Dipesh Chakrabarty argues, non-Western thought is consistently precluded from the constitution of knowledge proper. Third-world historians, as he writes:

> feel a need to refer to works in European history; historians of Europe do not feel any need to reciprocate . . . We cannot even afford an equality or symmetry of ignorance at this level without taking the risk of appearing 'old fashioned' or 'outdated' (Chakrabarty 1992, p. 2).

This absence of reciprocity is compounded when we consider that European philosophy has never allowed its cultural ignorance to qualify its claims of universality:

> For generations now, philosophers and thinkers shaping the nature of social science have produced theories embracing the entirety of humanity; as we well know, these statements have been produced in relative, and sometimes absolute, ignorance of the majority of humankind i.e., those living in non-Western cultures' (Chakrabarty 1992, p. 3).

Chakrabarty's arguments touch upon the heart of postcolonialism's quarrel with the orthodox humanities. However, while he restricts his focus to the problem of historical knowledge, postcolonial studies claims that the entire field of the humanities is vitiated by a compulsion to claim a spurious universality and also to disguise its political investment in the production of 'major' or 'dominant' knowledges. The epistemological and pedagogic reterritorialisation of the non-Western world thus involves a two-fold task: first, to expose the humanist pretence of political disinterestedness, and, second, to 'provincialise'—in Chakrabarty's terms—the knowledge claims of 'the "Europe" that modern imperialism and nationalism have, by their collaborative venture and violence, made universal' (Chakrabarty 1992, p. 20).

In order to assess the validity of this invective against the humanities we need now to cast a critical postcolonial eye upon the genealogy and formation of humanist knowledge—to return, as it were, to the first elaboration of the humanities as a privileged branch of study in sixteenth-century Florence.

Power, knowledge and the humanities

The term 'humanism' owes its origins to a secular and anthropocentric cultural and educational program concerned with the celebration and cultivation of 'human' achievements. The history of this pedagogic program is connected, in a circuitous way, to the emergence of an apparently new Italian word in the mid-sixteenth century, *umanista*, which comes to refer to the teacher, scholar or student engaged in that branch of studies known as the *studia humanitatis*, or generally speaking the liberal arts (see Campana 1946). The emergence of this word gestures toward the establishment of the liberal arts as a discipline within the academy—it marks the historical moment when the humanities became a special teaching subject at Italian universities, and relatedly, the monopoly of a certain group of specialists or academics. An academic discipline, as Paul Bove argues, is 'an accumulative, cooperative project for the production of knowledge, the exercise of power, and the creation of careers' (Bove 1985; cited in Spanos 1986, p. 52)—and the rise of the *umanista* in mid-sixteenth century Italy marks the process whereby a set of vested interests starts to attach itself to the promotion of the liberal arts.

Notably, while the term *umanista* can be traced to Renaissance Italy, the phrase *studia humanitatis* has a much earlier

Ciceronian etymology, and it carries within itself the notion of literary study as the only form of knowledge befitting a human being. As Cicero puts it, 'to live with the Muses means to live humanistically' (*Tusculan Disputations*, 5, 23, 66; cited in Curtius 1953, p. 228). Cicero's epistemological bias, in turn, evolves out of an even earlier consensus which, in Ernst Curtius' words, 'placed all higher intellectual pursuits under the sign of the Muses' (Curtius 1953, p. 230). Thus, Homer's *Iliad* praises the Muses for their knowledge of all things, and Virgil's Muses are consistently celebrated as the custodians of philosophy. Renaissance apologists for the *studia humanitatis* enthusiastically draw upon these multiple historical accretions, whereby poetry or literature are claimed as the foundation of all human knowledge. The Renaissance humanist Leonardo Bruni, for instance, defends the natural ascendancy of this new knowledge on the grounds that it is universal in its reach and, therefore, uniquely positioned to provide a complete education. In his words: 'the *litterae* are about to return with all their fertility, to form whole men, not just scholars. They call themselves *studia humanitatis* because they shape the perfect man' (see Garin 1965, p. 38).

Bruni's lavish praise of the humanities is significant for three reasons. First, like Cicero, he upholds the study of 'letters' for its capacity to produce 'whole' or representative human beings; second, his appeal to the ideas of 'forming' and 'shaping' delivers a specific understanding of pedagogic practice and thereby of the *umanista*'s professional role and function; and finally, by emphasising the relevance of the *studia humanitatis* to those who are 'not just scholars', he extends the function of humanistic education outside the academy. Each of these features in Bruni's plaudit points to limitations within human-ism which constitute the target of what we have been calling anti-humanist or oppositional criticism. In order to clarify these limitations we need to explore the field and consequences of Renaissance humanism more thoroughly.

To begin with, it is important to remember that the edu-cational program of the *studia humanitatis* was built upon a series of curricular exclusions, especially of those branches of study associated with medieval scholasticism. Accordingly, and despite its claims to representativeness, this program excluded—from the moment of its inception—a range of other academic fields such as logic, mathematics, the natural sciences, astronomy, medicine, law and theology. Broadly speaking, and as a variety of commentators have argued, the quarrel between humanism and scholasticism was essentially one between the so-called 'sciences of man' and the 'sciences of nature' (see Garin 1965, pp. 24–9). In the course of the ensuing debate, the humanists relentlessly claimed the moral high ground against the allegedly 'base' concerns of non-literary disciplines. Petrarch is characteristically and tellingly vitriolic on the subject:

> Carry out your trade, mechanic, if you can. Heal bodies, if you can. If you can't, murder; and take the salary for your crimes . . . But how can you dare, with unprecedented impertinence, to relegate rhetoric to a place inferior to medicine? How can you make a mistress inferior to the servant, a liberal art to a mechanical one? (See Garin 1965, p. 24.)

The hierarchy of knowledges proposed by Petrarch self-evidently draws upon corresponding markers of social hierarchy—the relationship of the liberal arts to the natural sciences is, accordingly, like that of the mistress to the servant. Thus, Petrarch complicates the humanist claim to representativeness both by excluding certain types of knowledge from the curricular boundaries of the *studia humanitatis* and also by hinting at categories of people (i.e. servants and mechanics) who might not be considered adequately or representatively human. Similar clues regarding the insidious exclusions of humanist knowledge inhere in his distinction between the 'liberal' and 'mechanical' arts and in the disparaging comment he addresses to murderous doctors—'take the salary for your crimes', which reinforces the social differentiation between the pure activity of 'artists' and the manual labour of 'artisans'.

It is also worth noting that Petrarch's separation of the liberal and mechanical domains is built upon a politically charged discrimination—especially resonant for postcolonial scholars—between civilised and barbaric cultural activity. The project of the *studia humanitatis*, as Heidegger points out in his 'Letter on humanism', has always relied on an opposition between the normative idea of humanistic man or *Homo humanus*, on the one hand, and the aberrant idea of barbaric man or *Homo barbarus*, on the other. In his words:

> *Humanitatis*, explicitly so called, was first considered and striven for in the age of the Roman Republic. *Homo humanus* was opposed to *Homo barbarus*. *Homo humanus* here means the Romans . . . whose culture was acquired in the schools of philosophy. It was concerned with . . . scholarship and training in good conduct (Heidegger 1977, p. 200).

Renaissance humanism takes over these discriminations from its Roman predecessors, and in so doing, it starts to reveal a fundamental contradiction at the heart of its project. While claiming the capacity to produce representative human beings, it imposes a series of cultural, social and economic constraints on the very quality of human-ness.

Seen in these terms, and once again through Foucault's hypothesis about dominant knowledge systems, the cultural and educational project of the *studia humanitatis*, can be seen to function, 'as a double repression: in terms of those whom it excludes from the process and in terms of the model and the standard (the bars) it imposes on those receiving this knowledge' (Foucault 1977, p. 219). Foucault's observation about the regulatory mechanisms of major knowledges brings us back to Bruni, whose praise of the humanities, it will be remembered, celebrated the *umanista*'s capacity to 'shape' and 'form' his students in a particular way. What exactly were these students being shaped into? And what does this concern with the formation of pedagogic subjects tell us about the humanistic claims to disinterestedness? Both of these questions have a direct bearing on the role of the humanities outside the academy—they point to what we might call the political motivations of the *studia humanitatis*.

In his recent book, *The Western Canon*, the critic Harold Bloom argues that the traditional humanities are politically unmotivated. The activity of reading, he insists, is solitary rather than social, and literature is, therefore, unlikely to provide a sound basis for social change: 'real reading is a lonely activity and does not teach anyone to become a better citizen' (Bloom 1994, p. 526). Although his arguments are often quite compelling, Bloom neglects to observe that humanism proper has consistently regarded literary education as a necessary apparatus for the proper functioning of the State. In other words, humanism has always functioned as an 'aesthetico-moral ideology' which is concerned with, and directed toward, the moulding of ideal citizen-subjects (see Cantimori 1934, p. 86). So, for example, the Florentine humanist Brucioli praises the liberal arts on the grounds that, 'only those disciplines are worthy of being called the best for the training of youth which are needed for the government of the Republic' (cited in Cantimori 1934, p. 97).

Furthermore, humanism, as we have seen, regarded itself as an academic and pedagogic pursuit of perfected human nature or *humanitas*. Accordingly, while proponents of humanism argued that this ideal human nature was embodied in, and expressed through, various forms of human activity and organisation—such as language and literature, the family and civic life—most humanists were of the opinion that the State was the archetypal and representative form of *humanitas*. Hence it followed, for writers like Brucioli, that the State should also be posed as the logical and proper end of all *studia humanitatis*. It is in this spirit that Bruni prefaces his translation of Aristotle's *Politics* with the assertion that:

> among the moral doctrines through which human life is shaped, those which refer to states and their governments occupy the highest position. For it is the purpose of those doctrines to make possible a happy life for all men . . . The more universal the well-being, the more divine it must be considered to be (see Garin 1965, p. 41).

Brucioli, likewise, sees the best examples of human nature embodied in those who have the capacity to command rather than obey. In his words, 'not all parts of the soul are of the same value, but some command while others obey, and those which command are best, so the Prince is the summit of the people . . .' (cited in Cantimori 1934, p. 93).

The Renaissance humanist valorisation of the State as the proper end of knowledge recurs in all subsequent manifestations of humanism. It is certainly a powerful component of the nineteenth-century humanist revival which occurs under the aegis of German idealism. Schiller's paradigmatic text, *Letters on the Aesthetic Education of Man*, for instance, recalls the Florentine reasoning we have been discussing, in its insistence that the primary objective of aesthetic education is the realisation of the rational State:

> Each individual human being, one might say, carries within him, potentially and prescriptively, an ideal man, the archetype of a human being, and it is his life's task to be, through all his changing manifestations, in harmony with the unchanging unity of this ideal. This archetype, which is to be discerned more or less clearly in every individual, is represented by the State, the objective and, as it were, the canonical form in which the diversity of individual subjects strive to unite (Schiller 1966, p. 17; cited in Lloyd 1985, p. 165).

For Schiller, as for his Renaissance predecessors, the State's canonicity derives from its capacity to embody the best and, therefore, the most representative qualities of human nature. The same idea is, of course, more famously reiterated in Matthew Arnold's 'Culture and Anarchy'. In Arnold's words, 'culture suggests the idea of the State. We find no basis for a firm State-power in our ordinary selves; culture suggests one to us in our best selves' (*Complete Prose Works*, vol. 5, p. 135).

In all its historical manifestations, humanist thought is clearly unified in its aspiration to establish a symbiotic relationship between culture—or knowledge—and the State. Nevertheless, the humanist attempt to make knowledge eternally amenable to power is almost always accompanied, as I have been suggesting, by corresponding protestations about the disinterestedness of humanist pedagogy. As Arnold insists in his 'The Function of Criticism at the Present Time':

the rule may be summed up in one word—disinterestedness. And how is criticism to show disinterestedness? By keeping aloof from what is called 'the practical view of things' . . . By steadily refusing to lend itself to any of those ulterior, political, practical considerations about ideas . . . (*Complete Prose Works*, vol. 3, pp. 269–70).

There are two observations to make in response to Arnold's rule of disinterestedness. First—like Seneca and Petrarch—Arnold uses the norm of disinterested inquiry to discredit all those allegedly 'ulterior', 'political' and 'practical' interests which, for one reason or another, pull away from, and are therefore unassimilable within, the dominant consensus represented in the State. The character and name of these disqualified interests have, of course, varied historically. Arnold identifies them within the uncultured and 'jealous' working classes—recognisably the descendants of Renaissance *meccanicos*. At other times, these discordant interests have been identified with numerous 'minority' groups, or with the ungovernable and uncivilised subjects of empire. Second, the Arnoldian appeal to disinterestedness effectively works to conceal the fact of the State's investment in the production of knowledge and culture—it serves to disguise the collaboration between knowledge and dominant interests. As a strategy, disinterestedness helps to bolster the State's fallacious claim to universality. In summary, as Marx and Engels argue, the ruling class is compelled 'to present its interest as the common interest of all members of society, that is, expressed in an ideal form: it has to give its ideas the form of universality, to present them as the only rational, universally valid ones' (Marx & Engels 1975, vol. 5, p. 60; cited in Guha 1992, p. 70).

In a final note on the collusion between humanism and the, albeit concealed, interests of the State, it is important to recognise that humanism has flourished whenever these established interests have been under threat or in need of reaffirmation. While we do not have the space here to detail the historical contiguity between various humanist and nation-alist revivals, it is worth mentioning that humanism has almost always accompanied and supported the emergence of unified and centralised nation-States. Thus, Italian humanism carries within it an appeal for some sort of unification among the Italian States, and the nineteenth-century German idealist ver-sion of humanism, likewise, communicates a call for the unification of Germany. So, also, Arnold's totalitarian human-ism expresses an anxiety about the potential anarchism of the wilful and uncontainable 'populace' at home, and abroad in the colonies. Arnold's humanism, in particular, asserts the need to maintain the integrity and sovereignty of Europe in the face of its multitudinous and barbaric Others.

Oppositional criticism and the new humanities

In view of the preceding discussion, we can now begin to summarise the motivations of the 'new humanities', or oppo-sitional and anti-humanist criticism. Edward Said echoes Foucault in his claim that such criticism must ideally, perhaps even impossibly, 'think of itself as life-enhancing and consti-tutively opposed to every form of tyranny, domination, and abuse; its social goals are non-coercive knowledge produced in the interests of human freedom' (Said 1983, p. 29). We might argue more specifically that an oppositional critical discourse like postcolonialism counters the exclusions of humanist thought through an attempt to make the field of knowledge more representative. This project relies upon two types of critical revelation or 'showing'. First, it takes upon itself the sometimes self-important function of revealing the interests which inhabit the production of knowledge. As Stuart Hall writes of the cultural studies project:

> . . . when cultural studies began its work . . . it had . . . to undertake the task of unmasking what it considered to be the unstated presuppositions of the humanist tradition itself. It had to bring to light the ideological assumptions underpinning the practice, to expose the educational program . . . and to

try and conduct an ideological critique of the way the humanities and the arts presented themselves as parts of disinterested
knowledge (Hall 1990b, p. 15).

Second, the investigative function of oppositional criticism
also draws attention to, and thereby attempts to retrieve, the
wide range of illegitimate, disqualified or subjugated knowledges mentioned earlier in this discussion. Habermas describes
this function as an 'emancipatory knowledge interest' which
'takes the historical traces of suppressed dialogue and recon-
structs what has been suppressed' (Habermas 1972, p. 315).
While Foucault also refers to this project in similar terms as
an attempt to achieve an insurrection of subjugated knowledges, he is sensitive to the dangers of a utopian desire simply
to invert the existing hierarchy of knowledges. A simple inversion, he maintains, will merely duplicate the institutions being
attacked and thereby constitute another orthodoxy—in this
case, the orthodoxy of heterodoxy: 'is it not perhaps the case
that these fragments of genealogies are no sooner brought to
light, that the particular elements of the knowledge that one
seeks to disinter are no sooner accredited and put into circulation, than they run the risk of re-codification, of
re-colonization' (Foucault 1980a, p. 86). Foucault's intervention compels oppositional criticism to contemplate the
difficulties of dissociating the recovery of subjugated knowledges from the will to power.

In this regard, Deleuze and Guattari suggest—somewhat
elusively—that subjugated knowledges and literatures must
resolutely replace the desire to become 'major' or canonical,
with an opposite dream: 'a becoming-minor' (Deleuze &
Guattari 1986, p. 27). Although the precise implications of
this project remain unclear, we might say that all 'minor'
knowledges need to retain the memory of their subjugation
and deterritorialisation and, therefore, of their creative affinity
with other fields of 'non-culture'. A more philosophically
complex version of this suggestion may be found in the
procedures of what Heidegger calls *Lichtung*. The word carries
within itself the double sense of 'light' and 'clearing'—it

designates a bringing to light which is also a clearing of space: 'In the midst of beings as a whole, there an open place occurs. There is a clearing, a lighting' (Halliburton, 1981, p. 43). Such is the illumination and expansiveness of Heideggarian *Lichtung* that it enables the most restrictive human consciousness to experience the simultaneity of the familiar and the uncanny, the established and the emergent, home and not-home, the humane and, equally, the barbaric. Seen in these terms, *Lichtung* is the reminder that identity is always underpinned by the presence of its Other, or that every major knowledge carries within itself the possibility of a countervailing minor-ness.

In its utopian mode, oppositional criticism aspires to the condition of Heidegger's *Lichtung*. Whether its aspirations are successful is, of course, another matter. But we can end this section with Kwame Anthony Appiah's suggestive claim that 'the post in postcolonial, like the post in postmodern is the post of a space clearing gesture . . .' (Appiah 1992, p. 240). In this postcolonial 'clearing'/*Lichtung* it might finally be possible to recognise the epistemological valency of non-European thought. Or, as Chakrabarty writes, in the newly liberated space of postcolonial pedagogy we might start to imagine '(infra)structural sites' where the dreams of provincialising Europe 'could lodge themselves' (Chakrabarty 1992, p. 23).

The world and the book

Postcolonialism, then, derives from the anti-humanism of poststructuralism and the 'new humanities' a view of Western power as a symptom of Western epistemology and pedagogy. And insofar as the postcolonial critique of colonial modernity is mapped out principally as an intervention into the realm of Western knowledge-production, it paves the way for a privileged focus on the revolutionary credentials of the postcolonial intellectual. Postcolonialism is not alone or eccentric in its bias toward academic activism—thinkers from within leftist traditions have always defended the public responsibilities of the intellectual figure. Antonio Gramsci, the Marxist Italian political philosopher, famously upheld the everyday social influence of the 'organic intellectual'. Althusser, the French pioneer of structural Marxism, likewise praised teachers for their resistance to the State ideology embedded within educational institutions. Similarly, Foucault's equation of knowledge and power confers a unique radicalism upon the dissident or oppositional thinker. Yet, notwithstanding these precedents, postcolonialism's investment in its intellectuals has been bitterly contested by its antagonists. While postcolonial theorists have attempted variously to defend the politics of their academic practice, recent critics of postcolonial theorising have asserted the unsustainable distance between the self-reflexive preoccupations of the postcolonial academy, on the one hand, and the concerns arising from, and relevant to, postcolonial realities, on the other.

Some vigilant and self-critical postcolonial theorists agree that the academic labour of postcolonialism is often blind to its own socially deleterious effect. Among this group, Gayatri Spivak is salutary in her warning that recent concessions to marginality studies within the first-world metropolitan academy inadvertently serve to identify, confirm, and thereby exclude certain cultural formations as chronically marginal (Spivak 1993, p. 55). The celebratory 'third worldism' of postcolonial studies, Spivak cautions, may well perpetuate real social and political oppressions which rely upon rigid distinctions between the 'centre' and the 'margin' (see 1993, p. 55). Spivak's warnings accrue, in part, from Foucault's paradigmatic resistance to the intellectual valorisation of marginality. As he argues:

> One must not suppose that there exists a certain sphere of 'marginality' that would be the legitimate concern of a free and disinterested scientific inquiry were it not the object of mechanisms of exclusion brought to bear by the economic or ideological requirements of power. If 'marginality' is being constituted as an area of investigation, this is only because relations of power have established it as a possible object . . .

(Foucault 1978, p. 98; cited with contextual modifications in Spivak 1993, p. 59).

Although both Foucault and Spivak contest the academic institutionalisation of 'marginality discourse', neither is willing to concede an absolute schism between intellectual activity and political realities. In sharp contrast, anti-postcolonial criticism repeatedly foregrounds the irresolvable dichotomy between the woolly deconstructive predicament of postcolonial intellectuals and the social and economic predicament of those whose lives are literally or physically on the margins of the metropolis. Critics like Arif Dirlik and Aijaz Ahmad, in particular, are unrelenting in their exclusion of all theoretical/intellectual activity which lacks adequate referents to 'everyday' sociality. Thus, Ahmad's recent article, 'The politics of literary postcoloniality', announces an ethical distinction between the tiresome domain of postcolonial literary theory and the con- siderably more 'fulsome debate on . . . the type of postcolonial states which arose in Asia and Africa after postwar decolonisations' (Ahmad 1995, p. 1).

This distinction is self-evidently premised upon the assump- tion that structural shifts in forms of governance affect more people more directly than imaginative shifts in critical meth- odologies. While Ahmad's claim is incontestable in itself, his objections take a disablingly prejudicial turn when he begins to treat all postcolonial theoretical practice as purely recrea- tional. In his reasoning, postcolonial theorising—indeed, all theorising outside the social sciences—is a luxury based upon the availability of 'mobility and surplus pleasure' to a privi- leged few, while the vast majority of others are condemned to labour 'below the living standards of the colonial period' (1995, pp. 16, 12). In other words, while postcolonial subjects must work to stay alive, postcolonial intellectuals are free to partake 'of a carnivalesque collapse and play of identities' (1995, p. 13). Ahmad's polemic—here, as elsewhere—is spe- cifically targeted against the postcolonial preoccupation with questions regarding the formation of subjectivities. As far as he is concerned, these self-indulgent and solipsistic questions abjure the 'real' politics of the collectivity. A similar bias appears in Arif Dirlik's article, 'The postcolonial aura: third world criticism in the age of global capitalism', which argues that the predominantly 'epistemological and psychic orientations of postcolonial intellectuals' are ethically incompatible with and irrelevant to the 'problems of social, political and cultural domination' (Dirlik 1994, p. 331).

Ahmad's and Dirlik's objections accrue from the recognition of a radical split between the 'private' and the 'public' realm of human/social experience. Fredric Jameson has accounted for this split in terms of a dichotomy 'between the poetic and the political, between what we have come to think of as the domain of sexuality and the unconscious and that of the public world of classes, of the economic, and of secular political power' (Jameson 1986, p. 69). Jameson's analysis points to a contestation which is fundamentally marked, as he acknowledges, by the theoretical distinctions between Freud and Marx. While this contestation has assumed a number of forms in a number of divergent contexts, it has been most clearly articulated in the theoretical differences between psychoanalytic and socialist feminists. Whereas psychoanalytic feminists have been primarily concerned with the formation and deformation of female subjectivity, their socialist adversaries have emphasised the singular importance of class identity, and concomitantly stigmatised the realm of 'feeling' as non-political and regressive (see Kaplan 1985). This prejudice against feeling is sustained partly by the assumption that the condition of 'interiority'— required by feeling —presupposes a receding away from the social into the narcissistic pleasures of fantasy and the imagination. Seen as such, the cult of feeling privileges individual desire over collective necessity, and the fulfilment of personal longings at the cost of social agency. Thus, female subjectivity comes to represent, in Kaplan's words, 'the site where the opposing forces of femininity and feminism clash by night' (Kaplan 1985, p. 154).

Dirlik and Ahmad, to turn the discussion once again to postcolonialism, rehearse this bias against 'inwardness' with one crucial difference. In their analysis it is the *intellectual* work and content of postcolonialism which comes to occupy the space, and thereby earn the stigma conventionally reserved for the luxury of 'feeling'. For both critics, postcolonial theorising is—like bourgeois interiority—a matter of class or, in this case, institutional privilege. According to Dirlik, for instance, postcolonialism happens 'when Third world intellectuals have arrived in the First world' (Dirlik 1994, p. 329).

Dirlik's metaphor of arrival—of 'having arrived'—is resonant with the charge of opportunism or 'having made it' in the first world; it implicitly predicates the professional success of postcolonial intellectuals upon a contingent and constitutive departure from the 'third world'. Seen in these terms, the postcolonial intellectual's journey becomes a flight from collective socialities—from the materiality of the beleaguered 'third world'—into the abstraction of metropolitan theory. For Dirlik, therefore, postcolonialism is not so much a description of a global condition, as a narrowly conceived 'label to describe academic intellectuals of Third world origin' (1994 p. 330). On a similar note, Ahmad's book-length polemic on postcolonial theory insists that postcolonial intellectuals are merely 'radicalised immigrants located in the metropolitan university', who are uniformly marked by a 'combination of class origin, professional ambition and a lack of prior political grounding in socialist praxis' (Ahmad 1992, p. 86). Seen through this glass, and darkly, the postcolonial intellectual emerges as a travelling theorist who has, in the manner of Rushdie's buoyant migrant 'floated upward from history'.

The postcolonial intellectual

While there is much to learn from Ahmad's and Dirlik's vigil against 'an opportunistic kind of Third-Worldism' (Ahmad 1992, p. 86), we need to guard against their generalising assumption that any attempt to think the 'third world' from the 'first' is bound to maintain, in Ahmad's words, 'only an ironic relation with the world and its intelligibility' (1992, 36). From another perspective, their objections can be invoked—

more usefully—to interrogate the incommensurability between the oppositional stance of postcolonial intellectuals and their co-option within the very institutions they allegedly critique. As Cornel West argues, all cultural critics who attempt to contest the operations of power within their own institutional contexts find themselves in a disabling double bind: 'while linking their activities to the fundamental, structural overhaul of these institutions, they often remain financially dependent on them . . . For these critics of culture, theirs is a gesture that is simultaneously progressive and coopted' (West 1990, p. 94).

The problem of 'positionality' accordingly devolves upon the progressive intellectual the task of continually resisting the institutional procedures of co-option—such an intellectual must relentlessly negotiate the possibility of being, in Spivak's elusive terminology, 'outside in the teaching machine'. The task becomes more urgent when we reconsider Foucault's and Spivak's warnings about the centre's parasitic relationship to the margin. Neocolonialism, as Spivak reminds us, 'is fabricating its allies by proposing a share of the centre in a seemingly new way (not a rupture but a displacement): disciplinary support for the conviction of authentic marginality by the (aspiring) elite' (Spivak 1993, p. 57). Spivak's statement indirectly raises a number of open-ended questions: can postcolonialism be ethically professed only from within allegedly 'postcolonial' locations? Should third-world intellectuals in the first-world academy restrict their study to mainstream culture? Is it possible to disseminate marginalised knowledges without monumentalising the condition(s) of marginality? And finally, if facetiously, do intellectuals count anyway?

It is appropriate, in the context of these queries, to consider that, subsequent to the 'explosion' of marginality studies, the first-world academy is now involved, as Spivak puts it, 'in the construction of a new object of investigation—"the third world", "the marginal"—for institutional validation and certification' (1993, p. 56). Far from being disinterested, this investigation testifies, in many ways, to the persisting Western interest in the classification, analysis and production of what we might call 'exotic culture'. And to this end, it relies upon the dubious good offices of the native (intellectual) informant.

In recent years, the problem of the native intellectual as a native informant has been forcefully posed within the United States. academy through the intervention of a wide variety of 'internally colonised' or 'minority' communities. Among these, Chicana/o communities have been prominent in their conflictual engagement with the role and function of 'ethnic' intellectual/academic representatives. The work of a writer like Angie Chabran, for instance, is informed by the anxiety that the Chicana/o intellectual—indeed, the whole enterprise of Chicana/o studies—uncritically assists in the anthropologisation of the Chicana/o people (Chabran 1990). Rosaura Sanchez elaborates this anxiety by pointing to the insidious relationship between the apparently neutral field of 'area studies' and the considerably more biased field of 'public policy'. 'The state interest in gathering information', Sanchez contends, 'calls for the establishment of academic programs that can oversee a systematic and complex collection of data as well as interpret it for decision makers in this society' (Sanchez 1990, p. 299).

While these critics are necessarily alert to the covert operations of governmentality within the academy, their misgivings—much as those of Dirlik and Ahmad—often result in a categorical mistrust of intellectual activity in and of itself. In an argument which questions the fetishisation of intellectual authority, Chabran, for instance, reasserts the primacy of experience over theory. She appeals to the instructive status of the intellectuals' pre-institutional history in the fields, the family and the factory, on the grounds that we have to consider 'the shaping way in which experience directs us to ask certain questions of [a] particular theory which theory alone does not lead us to ask' (Chabran 1990, p. 242). Despite its irrefutable good sense, Chabran's claim leaves two questions unanswered. First, is experience the only valid precondition for theory? If so, and second, can one then speak about anything which is outside one's realm of experience? In other words, can a white intellectual profess a valid interest in non-white communities, or a heterosexual intellectual in gay communities, or, for that matter, a contemporary intellectual in medieval communities? Taken to an extreme, the unilateral privileging of experience over theory—or activism over the academy—works to disqualify or debar the social validity of almost all intellectual activity.

Thus, while a critic like Mike Featherstone proscribes the activities of literary intellectuals on the grounds that 'we have to raise the sociological objection against the literary intellectual's license in interpreting the everyday, or in providing evidence about everyday lives of ordinary people' (Featherstone 1988, pp. 199–200), Iain Chambers celebrates the experiential complexity of the contemporary world for its total dissolution of the vainglorious intellect. 'A certain intellectual formation', in his words, 'is discovering that it is losing its grip on the world' (Chambers 1987, p. 20).

This resurgence of anti-intellectualism within leftist thinking is distressing when we consider that right-wing governments and lobbies are also engaged in the ruthless excision of intellectual work from national and budgetary agendas. Painfully, we seem to have inherited a world where, as John Frow argues, both the left and the right seem to collude in their objections to non-utilitarian activity. In his words:

> The problem is most deeply that of the possible place of critical thought in a capitalist society—that is, in a society that seeks to harness knowledge more or less directly to the generation of profit. Whereas once we could envisage spaces of exception to the logic of capital accumulation, these ethical and aesthetic spaces are disappearing in the face of a more totalizing rationality. One indication of this is the way in which, in the discourses both of the New Right and of their near cousins the technocratic left, an economic vocabulary is used to discredit the study of the humanities (Frow 1990, p. 357).

Utilitarianism, as Frow points out, has a variety of liberal and illiberal manifestations. At either extreme, however, it is marked by a reverence for the notion of quantifiable or visible effects. For left-thinking utilitarian critics, furthermore, visibility is seen to be the exclusive preserve of experience or praxis, and theory suffers by contrast as its effects are neither immediately apparent nor quantifiable. Ironically, the current anti-intellectual bias within the left is entirely out of step with Marxism's long-standing insistence on the necessary coalition between thought and everyday life.

It is instructive here to recall Raymond Williams' understanding of culture as 'whole way of life' within which artistic and intellectual labour coexist through necessary linkages with other social activities (Williams 1981, p. 10–14). Williams' concession to the thought content of any given social order also appears—although from often entirely divergent positions—within the work of Habermas and Foucault. Habermas, for instance, argues that the schism between the contrary realms of purely empirical and purely transcendental knowledges is invariably mediated by those forms of knowing which are essential to the cultural reproduction of social life. These mediating knowledges, which he calls 'cognitive interests', refer to the complex processes of learning and mutual understanding which always accompany the activities of work and interaction. Knowledge, he argues, does not have to be either 'a mere instrument of an organism's adaptation to a changing environment nor the act of a pure rational being removed from the context of life in contemplation' (Habermas 1972, p. 197). Habermas undoes the demarcation between knowledge and human interest by postulating cognition as a necessary effect of social life. Foucault takes this proposition a step further by shifting the focus from knowledge to the question of thought itself, so as to argue that all forms of activity—of doing—are always informed, if not produced, by forms of thinking. Foucault's interest in making this claim is motivated by a definitive resistance to the idea that social life is necessarily more real and therefore more relevant than the activity of thought:

> We must free ourselves from the sacrilization of the social as the only reality and stop regarding as superfluous something so essential in human life as thought. Thought exists independently of systems and structures of discourse. It is something that is often hidden, but which always animates

everyday behaviour. There is always a little thought even in the most stupid institutions (Foucault 1989, p. 155).

There are serious limitations, as Foucault tells us, to a critique of academic activism which insists upon the fundamental irrelevance of all knowledge production. The intellectual's armchair is, indeed, a considerably less hazardous—and possibly less effective—political location than the revolutionary battleground. Even so, it remains a crucial sphere of influence—a place from which it is possible both to agitate thought within 'stupid institutions' and also, as Foucault maintains, to propose 'an insurrection of knowledges that are opposed . . . to the effects of the centralising powers that are linked to the institution' (Foucault 1980a, p. 84). If the postcolonial intellectual has a political vocation, then it inheres, as we have been arguing, in a commitment to facilitate a democratic dialogue between the Western and non-Western academies, and in so doing, to think a way out of the epistemological violence of the colonial encounter. But equally, this commitment comes with an infrequently heeded obligation of humility. Despite the protestations of some postcolonial critics, postcolonial theory speaks to a very limited constituency and, as Dirlik and Ahmad insist, there is always more to politics than theory.

4

Edward Said and his critics

The principal features of postcolonialism's intellectual inheritance—which we covered in the preceding two chapters—are realised and elaborated in Edward Said's *Orientalism* (1991, first published in 1978). Here, as elsewhere in his extensive oeuvre, Said betrays an uneasy relationship with Marxism, a specifically poststructuralist and anti-humanist understanding of the contiguity between colonial power and Western knowledge, and a profound belief in the political and worldly obligations of the postcolonial intellectual. This chapter will provide some contexts for understanding the canonisation of this book as a postcolonial classic through a consideration of its academic influence and theoretical limitations.

Enter Orientalism

Commonly regarded as the catalyst and reference point for postcolonialism, *Orientalism* represents the first phase of postcolonial theory. Rather than engaging with the ambivalent condition of the colonial aftermath—or indeed, with the history and motivations of anti-colonial resistance—it directs attention to the discursive and textual production of colonial meanings and, concomitantly, to the consolidation of colonial hegemony. While 'colonial discourse analysis' is now only one aspect of postcolonialism, few postcolonial critics dispute its enabling effect upon subsequent theoretical improvisations.

Gayatri Spivak, for example, has recently celebrated Said's book as the founding text or 'source book' through which 'marginality' itself has acquired the status of a discipline in the Anglo-American academy. In her words, 'the study of colonial discourse, directly released by work such as Said's, has . . . blossomed into a garden where the marginal can speak and be spoken, even spoken for. It is an important part of the discipline now' (Spivak 1993, p. 56). The editors of the influential Essex symposia series on the sociology of literature also invoke the spirit of Spivak's extravagant metaphor to argue that Said's pioneering efforts have single-handedly moved matters of colony and empire 'centre stage in Anglo-American literary and cultural theory . . .' (Barker et al. 1994, p. 1).

While these accounts testify to the valency of Said's dense text in the metropolitan Western academy, others eagerly confirm his influence on the 'third world' academy. Zakia Pathak, Saswati Sengupta and Sharmila Purkayasta have written passionately about the long awaited and messianic arrival of *Orientalism* into the alienated and alienating English Studies classroom in Delhi University. Said's *Orientalism*, they claim, finally taught them how to teach a literature which was not their own:

> To deconstruct the text, to examine the process of its production, to identify the myths of imperialism structuring it, to show how the oppositions on which it rests are generated by political needs at given moments in history, quickened the text to life in our world (Pathak et al. 1991, p. 195).

A similar mood informs Partha Chatterjee's assessment of Said's book in terms of its impact on his own intellectual formation as a 'postcolonial' historian. His essay nostalgically recalls a revelatory first reading of *Orientalism* through an uncertain season in Calcutta:

I will long remember the day I read *Orientalism* . . . For me, child of a successful anti-colonial struggle, *Orientalism* was a book which talked of things I felt I had known all along but had never found the language to formulate with clarity. Like many great books it seemed to say to me for the first time what one had always wanted to say (Chatterjee 1992, p. 194).

Each of the accounts I have been citing attempts, in a different way, to postulate Said's book as a canonical 'event', and while Spivak and the editors of the Essex symposia series measure its canonicity in terms of its public and disciplinary impact, Chatterjee invites us to participate vicariously in the intellectual frisson of a private encounter between an uninitiated reader and a great book. Taken together, these appraisals decisively testify to *Orientalism*'s revolutionary impact on intellectual formations, structures and lives, both in the West and in the postcolonial non-West. There are, of course, a host of other more discontented critics who have remained impervious to the cognitive charms of this book, and who have contested its phenomenal status and pre-eminence. Nevertheless, as Tim Brennan asks of Said's detractors: 'Why . . . was it *Orientalism* . . . that changed the drift of scholarship in several disciplines, found readers in a number of languages, crept into the most unlikely footnotes, and inspired a feature-length film?' (Brennan 1992, p. 78). Before addressing these questions directly we might briefly summarise some of the themes and concerns of this volume.

Orientalism is the first book in a trilogy devoted to an exploration of the historically imbalanced relationship between the world of Islam, the Middle East, and the 'Orient' on the one hand, and that of European and American imperialism on the other. While *Orientalism* focuses on the well-rehearsed field of nineteenth-century British and French imperialism, the two subsequent books in this series, *The Question of Palestine* (1979) and *Covering Islam* (1981) foreground the submerged or latent imperialism which informs the relationship between Zionism and Palestine and that of the United States and the Islamic world.

Said's critics claim that these books are unremarkable in

the fact of their attention to the violence of imperialism. Insofar as they engage in an extended critique of imperial procedures, they are simply more updated versions of a well-established tradition of anti-colonial polemic which, as Aijaz Ahmad writes, is 'virtually as old as colonialism itself' (Ahmad 1992, p. 174). We have already encountered some early and significantly more contentious versions of this tradition in Gandhi and Fanon. What, then, is the particular contribution of *Orientalism* and its sequels to the defiant counter-hegemonic chorus of its predecessors? How do Said's books diagnose the Western will to power differently? Initially, we might say that the *Orientalism* series as a whole elaborates a unique understanding of imperialism/colonialism as the epistemological and cultural attitude which accompanies the curious habit of dominating and, whenever possible, ruling distant territories. As Said writes in his recent book *Culture and Imperialism*:

> Neither imperialism nor colonialism is a simple act of accumulation and acquisition. Both are supported and perhaps even impelled by impressive ideological formations which include notions that certain territories and people *require* and beseech domination, as well as forms of knowledge affiliated with that domination (Said 1993, p. 8).

Orientalism is the first book in which Said relentlessly unmasks the ideological disguises of imperialism. In this regard, its particular contribution to the field of anti-colonial scholarship inheres in its painstaking, if somewhat overstated, exposition of the reciprocal relationship between colonial knowledge and colonial power. It proposes that 'Orientalism'—or the project of teaching, writing about, and researching the Orient—has always been an essential cognitive accompaniment and inducement to Europe's imperial adventures in the hypothetical 'East'. Accordingly, it claims that the peculiarly 'Western style for dominating, restructuring, and having authority over the Orient' (Said 1991 [1978], p. 3) is inextricable from the peculiarly Western style of studying and thinking about the Orient. In other words, its answer to the way the East was won suggests that we reconsider some of the ways in which the East was known.

The Said phenomenon

In order properly to assess the phenomenal success of *Orientalism*, we need to return to the scene of its publication in 1978. Books, as Said insists in his collection of essays entitled, *The World, the Text and the Critic*, should be judged in terms of their circumstantiality or their implication in the social and political imperatives of the world in which they are produced. As he writes: 'My position is that texts are worldly, to some degree they are events, and, even when they appear to deny it, they are nevertheless a part of the social world, human life, and of course the historical moments in which they are located and interpreted' (Said 1983, p. 4). In subsequent works, such as *Culture and Imperialism*, Said develops this position further to argue that while all texts are 'worldly', great texts or 'masterpieces' encode the greatest pressures and preoccupations of the world around them. They successfully reveal and formalise prevailing structures of attitude and reference and, in so doing, indicate both the possibilities and the limits of these structures.

Raymond Williams makes a similar point in his very useful distinction between 'indicative' or 'subjunctive' texts. Whereas the former simply indicate what is happening in the world, the latter, he argues, gesture toward a radical perspective or impulse which is neither socially nor politically available, nor, for that matter, entirely permissible within the prevailing social order. Thus, 'subjunctive' texts are always 'attempting to lift certain pressures, to push back certain limits; and at the same time, in a fully extended production, bearing the full weight of the pressures and limits, in which the simple forms, the simple contents, of mere ideological reproduction can never achieve' (Williams 1986, p. 16). How far do Said's and Williams' criteria for canonicity apply to *Orientalism*? Is it possible, or even appropriate, to think of it as a radically 'subjunctive' text?

Said's detractors have implicitly invoked the logic of Williams' distinction between 'indicative' and 'subjunctive' texts to insist that *Orientalism* is utterly, even boringly, symptomatic and indicative of what was happening in the Anglo-American academy in the late 1970s and early 1980s. These critics insist that the academic world of Said's book was still recovering from the cataclysmic events of 1968. As is now well known, this date commemorates the accidents of a utopian revolution which swept across Europe, bringing workers and students together in a combined and unprecedented offensive against authoritarian educational institutions and the capitalist state. The agitation, of course, spluttered to a pathetic end on the streets of Paris—partly due to the disorganised character of the offensive itself, and partly due to the betrayal of the movement by its Stalinist leaders. The failures of 1968 brought in their wake a serious and disillusioned reconsideration of Marxist theory and its omissions. To some extent, this reconsideration was articulated, as we saw in the previous chapter, through poststructuralism—a theoretical enterprise which acquired academic prominence in the period directly leading up to the publication of *Orientalism*.

Few critics dispute the continuities between poststructuralist theory and *Orientalism*. While some have attempted sympathetically to historicise the extent of Said's debts to, and departures from, his theoretical predecessors, others have chosen to hold poststructuralism against him. Thus, for critics like Aijaz Ahmad, poststructuralism and its inheritors are unforgivably implicated in the demise of Marxist thinking. The reactionary content of poststructuralist theory, Ahmad maintains, is confirmed when we consider that its perverse ascent to dominance has been accompanied by the rise of right-wing governments and movements throughout the Anglo-American world. Thus, Reaganism, Thatcherism, the defeat of social democracy in Germany and Scandinavia, and the conservative backlash in France are all said to provide the definitive backdrop to the theoretical mal-condition of the Anglo-American academy in the late 1970s. Ahmad also argues that in the absence of any serious or legitimate 'leftist' thought, most intellectuals of this reactionary era guiltily took refuge in token and flabby forms of ecologism and 'third worldism'. In his words:

> The characteristic posture of this new intellectual was that he or she would gain legitimacy on the Left by fervently referring to the Third World, Cuba, national liberation, and so on, but would also be openly and contemptuously anti-communist; would often enough not only not affiliate even with that other tradition which had also descended from classical Marxism, namely social democracy, nor be affiliated in any degree with any labour movement whatsoever, but would invoke an anti-bourgeoisie stance in the name of manifestly reactionary anti-humanisms enunciated in the Nietzchean tradition and propagated now under the signature of anti-empiricism, anti-historicism, structuralism and post-structuralism . . . (Ahmad 1992, p. 192).

The objective of Ahmad's polemic, in this instance, is to provide a context for *Orientalism*. Insofar as he believes that the late 1970s were a misguidedly anti-Marxist, viciously poststructuralist and sentimentally tree-hugging and third-worldist time, he also believes that Said's book is entirely—and in Raymond Williams' sense of the word—'indicative' of this ethos. There is great substance in Ahmad's specific objections to *Orientalism*, but there is also reason to argue that in his account of the circumstantiality of this book, he protests a little too much. Although Said's text exhibits all the limits and constraints of its historically specific relation to Marxism, poststructuralism and the third world, it is also able to push against these structural and formal limits in interestingly 'subjunctive' ways.

Let us start by addressing the question of Marxism. Ever since the writing of *Orientalism*, Said has been consistently critical about the epistemological and ontological insufficiency of Marxist theory. His objections in this regard have been informed by a refusal to modify specific acts of criticism or politics in advance through labels like 'Marxism' or 'liberalism'. Criticism, as he writes, is most like itself 'in its suspicion of totalising concepts, in its discontent with reified objects, in its impatience with guilds, special interests, imperialised fiefdoms, and orthodox habits of mind' (Said 1983, p. 29). Said's account of critical/political activity advocates a movement away from premeditated systems of knowledge toward heterogeneous 'events' or acts of knowing. This is, of course, very similar to Lyotard's—and to an extent, Foucault's—disavowal of any intellectual or ethical subscription to totality. And, indeed, there is no doubt that Said's *general* objections to Marxist orthodoxy are historically mediated by the poststructuralist and postmodernist incredulity toward universalising and totalising 'grand narratives'. At the same time, and unlike Foucault and Lyotard, his *specific* disenchantment with Marxism is not occasioned by the experiences of 1968, which, as Terry Eagleton puts it, produced a violent reaction against 'all forms of political theory and organisation which sought to analyse, and act upon, the structures of society as a whole. For it was precisely such politics which seemed to have failed' (Eagleton 1983, p. 142). For Said, somewhat differently, the radical failure of Marxist categories arises from his perception of their inability to accommodate the specific political needs and experiences of the colonised world. As he says with reference to the Palestinian experience, 'the development of a theoretical marxism in the Arab world did not seem to meet adequately the challenges of imperialism, the formation of a nationalist elite, the failure of the national revolution' (see Sprinker 1992, p. 261). In *Orientalism*, Said substantiates the cultural inadequacy of Marxist theory by drawing attention to the blindness of Marx himself to the world outside Europe.

Marx, as is well known, defends the emergence and spread of European capitalist or bourgeois society as the universal precondition for social revolution. In this context, he identifies European colonialism as the historical project which facilitates the globalisation of the capitalist mode of production and, thereby, the destruction of 'backward' or pre-capitalist forms of social organisation. In many of Marx's writings, specifically his 1853 journalistic analyses of British rule in India, there is, thus, an implicit link between the progressive role of capital and the progressive role of colonialism. As Marx writes: 'England has to fulfil a double role in India: one destructive, the other regenerative—the annihilation of the Asiatic society and the laying of the material foundations of Western society in Asia' (Marx 1973, p. 320; cited in Said 1991 [1978], p. 154). Said responds to this pronouncement by arguing that the Marxist thesis on socioeconomic revolution is ultimately and ethically flawed from the perspective of the colonised world—first, because its vision of progress tiredly reiterates nineteenth-century assumptions of the fundamental inequality between East and West; and second, because it views the colonised 'Orient' simply as the abstract illustration of a theory rather than an existential mass of suffering individuals. And finally, it is inadequate because Marx follows the insidious logic of the colonial civilising mission in postulating Europe as the hyperreal master-narrative, which will pronounce the redemption of poor Asia. Thus, even socialism, as Fanon writes, becomes 'part of the prodigious adventure of the European spirit' (Fanon 1990, p. 253). Or, to put this differently, colonialism becomes a practical and theoretical exigency for the fulfilment of Marx's emancipatory vision.

Said's critique of Marxist theory arrives at a poststructuralist destination insofar as it demonstrates, once again, the always-already complicity of Western knowledges with the operative interests of Western power. And yet, the geographical and cultural parameters for Said's poststructuralist 'demonstration' are, as I have been arguing, radically different from those deployed by Foucault and Derrida in their revisionist critique of Western epistemology and cultural hegemony. For while these poststructuralist luminaries challenge the conceptual boundaries of the West from within Western culture, they are, as Homi Bhabha writes, notoriously and self-consciously ethnocentric in their refusal to push these boundaries 'to the colonial periphery; to that limit where the west must face a peculiarly displaced and decentred image of itself "in double duty bound", at once a civilising mission and a violent subjugating force' (Bhabha 1986, p. 148). Thus, while Derrida brilliantly details the *internal* inadequacies, betrayals and eli-sions of what he calls the system of 'Western metaphysics', he neglects adequately to theorise those *external* factors or civilisational Others which render this system unalienably 'Western'. So also, Foucault's scrupulous attention to the dis-cursive structure and order of Western civilisation remains culturally myopic with regard to the non-European world.

In this context, *Orientalism* needs to be read as an attempt to extend the geographical and historical terrain for the poststructuralist discontent with Western epistemology. It argues that in order to fully understand the emergence of the 'West' as a structure and a system we have also to recognise that the colonised 'Orient' has 'helped to define Europe as its contrasting image, idea, personality, experience' (Said 1991 [1978], p. 2). Thus, Said's critical pursuit of Marx out of the streets of Paris into Asia is symptomatic of the way in which his work, to quote Homi Bhabha again:

> dramatically shifts the locus of contemporary theory from the Left Bank to the West Bank and beyond, through a profound meditation on the myths of Western power and knowledge which confine the colonised and dispossessed to a half-life of misrepresentation and migration (Bhabha 1986, p. 149).

In conclusion, it would falsify Said's project if we simply attributed his critique of Marxism to his blind adherence to poststructuralism. For as we have seen, his objections to Marxism are fundamentally similar to his objections to poststructuralism. Both turn on the sense that these otherwise mutually antagonistic theories are in fact united in their ten-dency toward a crippling ethnocentrism. Having said this, we need also to recognise that Said is, as his critics point out, disablingly impervious to the accomplishment and value of the theories and knowledges he chooses to critique. He tends to underestimate his own intellectual debt to his poststructuralist predecessors and, perhaps more dangerously, fails to engage with the enormous contribution of Marxism to the 'third world'. Marxism, despite Said's objections, is not so much *complicit* with imperialism as it is an *account of* the necessary complicity of capitalism and colonialism. What it delivers theoretically, is a set of categories that we can work with, through which we might understand ourselves—and our implication in the history of capitalist/European imperialism—differently (see Chakrabarty 1993, pp. 421–3). Moreover, and as Gayatri Spivak repeatedly argues, it is profoundly enabling and useful to rethink the present relationship between the 'third' and 'first' worlds through Marxist accounts of the globalisation of capital and the international division of labour. As she argues, Marxist thought relies on the:

> possibility of suggesting to the worker that the worker produces capital because the worker, the container of labour power, is the source of value. By the same token it is possible to suggest to the so called 'Third World' that it *produces* the wealth and the possibility of the cultural self-representation of the 'First World' (Spivak 1990, p. 96).

In other words, it is possible to arrive at the conclusions of Said's *Orientalism* without necessarily debunking the entire project of Marxist epistemology. Then again, it is only with hindsight, only after *Orientalism*, that postcolonial scholars and theorists have been able to imagine the seemingly impossible collusion of poststructuralist scepticism with Marxist historicism.

Rethinking colonial discourse

I have been arguing that *Orientalism, The Question of Palestine* and *Covering Islam* each extend Foucault's paradigmatic account of the alliance between power and knowledge to colonial conditions. Foucault, as we have seen, explores the contiguity of power and knowledge in order to explicate the ways in which knowledge transforms power, changing it from a monolithic apparatus accumulated within the State into a web-like force which is confirmed and articulated through the everyday exchanges of 'know how' or information which animate social life. Accordingly, as Sneja Gunew writes, power 'is reproduced in discursive networks at every point where someone who "knows" is instructing someone who doesn't know' (Gunew 1990, p. 22). While Said listens carefully to Foucault's influential account of power, he is ultimately more interested in questions of knowledge or—more specifically—in exploring and critiquing the conditions under which knowledge might be transformed and vitiated through the contagion of power. Here Said seems to invoke the anarchist maxim that power corrupts to argue that power is especially corrupting when it comes into contact with knowledge. This, as he tells us, is the lesson to be learnt from *Orientalism*:

> If this book has any future use, it will be . . . as a warning: that systems of thought like Orientalism, discourses of power, ideological fictions—mind-forg'd manacles—are all too easily made, applied and guarded . . . If the knowledge of Orientalism has any meaning, it is in being a reminder of the seductive degradation of knowledge, of any knowledge, anywhere, at any time. Now perhaps more than before (Said 1991 [1978], p. 328).

Said's concern for the deleterious effect of power on knowledge elaborates his conviction that intellectual and cultural activity does, and should, improve the social world in which it is conducted. Nowhere does Said eschew the 'worldliness' or political texture of human knowledges. His introduction to *Orientalism* labours to refuse the distinction between 'pure' and 'political' knowledge on the grounds that no self-respecting scholar or writer can ethically disclaim their involvement in the actuality of their circumstances. Thus, knowledge is most like itself when it undertakes to counter and oppose the unequal distribution of power in the 'world'. It belongs, as Said writes, 'in that potential space inside civil society, acting on behalf of those alternative acts and alternative intentions whose advancement is a fundamental human and intellectual obligation' (Said 1983, p. 30). Likewise, knowledge is least like itself when it becomes institutionalised and starts to collaborate with the interests of a dominant or ruling elite. Said takes Orientalism as a paradigmatic instance of institutionalised and 'degraded' knowledge, to be opposed through an adversarial or oppositional counter-knowledge. His analysis of this field is built upon three fairly idiosyncratic 'meanings' of 'Orientalism', which he supplies at the beginning of his book. First, Said invokes the conventional understanding of 'Orientalism' as a field of specialisation or academic pursuit of the Orient. Strictly speaking, 'Orientalism' designates the pioneering efforts of eighteenth-century scholars and enthusiasts of Oriental cultures—such as William Jones, Henry T. Colebrooke and Charles Wilkins—who undertook the first translations of texts like the *Bhagavad Gita, Shakuntala* and portions of the *Upanishads*. Said is somewhat more liberal in his view that 'Orientalism' includes the activities of *any* professional Western academic—historian, sociologist, anthropologist, area studies expert or philologist—currently or previously engaged in studying, researching or teaching the 'Orient'. Second, he abandons the disciplinary confines of Orientalist tradition to argue, rather expansively, that Orientalism also refers to any, and every, occasion when a Westerner has either imagined or written about the non-Western world. So Orientalism becomes an imaginative cast of mind or style of thought which covers roughly two millennia of Western consciousness about the East. Homer, Aeschylus, Dante are all, by this reasoning, rebaptised as Orientalists. Third, Said finally delivers his principal understanding of 'Orientalism' as an enormous system or inter-textual network of rules and procedures which regulate anything that may be thought, written or imagined about the Orient. It is clear that this third description subsumes the first and the second meanings of 'Orientalism'. It also marks the historical juncture at which any Western attempt to 'know' or directly engage with the non-Western world is mediated, as James Clifford argues, by a tendency to *dichotomise* the relationship between the 'Occident' and the 'Orient' into an us–them contrast, and then, to *essentialise* the resultant 'Other'; to speak, that is, in a generalising way about the Oriental 'character', 'mind' and so on (Clifford 1988, p. 258).

In effect, Said's final description delivers an understanding of Orientalism as a *discourse*—in Foucault's sense of the term.

Sociolinguistic theory tells us that discourses, or discursive formations, are always linked to the exercise of power. They are modes of utterance or systems of meaning which are both constituted by, and committed to, the perpetuation of dominant social systems. In every society, as Foucault writes, 'the production of discourse is at once controlled, selected, organised and redistributed by certain numbers of procedures whose role is to ward off its dangers, to gain mastery over its chance events, to evade its ponderous, formidable materiality' (Foucault 1987, p. 52). Discourses are, in point of fact, heavily policed cognitive systems which control and delimit both the mode and the means of *representation* in a given society. Accordingly, colonial/Orientalist discourses are typical of discursive activity whenever they claim the right to *speak for* the mute and uncomprehending Orient and, in so doing, relentlessly represent it as the negative, underground image or impoverished 'Other' of Western rationality. In other words, Orientalism becomes a discourse at the point at which it starts systematically to produce stereotypes about Orientals and the Orient, such as the heat and dust, the teeming marketplace, the terrorist, the courtesan, the Asian despot, the child-like native, the mystical East. These stereotypes, Said tells us, confirm the necessity and desirability of colonial government by endlessly confirming the positional superiority of the West over the positional inferiority of the East. What they deliver, in his words, is the unchanging image of 'a subject race, dominated by a race that knows them and what is good for them better than they could possibly know themselves' (Said 1991 [1978], p. 35).

Said's project has been exemplary in its protest against the representational violence of colonial discourse and, indeed, in its commitment to the onerous task of consciousness raising in the Western academy. At the same time, *Orientalism* is often theoretically naive in its insistence that the Orientalist stereotype invariably presupposes and confirms a totalising and unified imperialist discourse. Accordingly, a wide variety of recent critics have revisited *Orientalism* to argue that cultural stereotypes are considerably more ambivalent and dynamic than Said's analysis allows. Homi Bhabha, in particular, argues that the negative Orientalist stereotype is an unstable category which marks the conceptual limit of colonial presence and identity. It is fundamentally threatening as the banished or underground 'Other' of the European self, and insofar as it embodies the contradictory expulsions of colonial fantasy and phobia, it actualises a potentially disruptive site of pleasure and anxiety. In Bhabha's words:

> Stereotyping is not only the setting up of a false image which becomes the scapegoat of discriminatory practices. It is a much more ambivalent text of projection and introjection, meta-phoric and metonymic strategies, displacement, guilt, aggressivity; the masking and splitting of 'official' and fantas-mic knowledges . . . (Bhabha 1986, p. 169).

Bhabha's psychoanalytically informed claims about the inderterminate and explosive structure of the colonial stereo-type are complemented by a growing critical awareness about the historically radical uses of Orientalism—both within the West and within the colonised non-West. Scholars such as Richard Fox and Partha Chatterjee argue that anti-colonial nationalist movements regularly drew upon affirmative Orien-talist stereotypes to define an authentic cultural identity in opposition to Western civilisation. Gandhian cultural resis-tance, Fox argues, typically 'depended upon an Orientalist image of India as inherently spiritual, consensual, and corpo-rate' (Fox 1992, p. 151). Correspondingly, enthusiastic Indian nationalists responded to perjorative stereotypes about India's caste-dominated, other-worldly, despotic and patriarchal social structure with reformist zeal and agency. Thus, Orientalist discourse was strategically available not only to the empire but also to its antagonists. Moreover, the affirmative stereotypes attached to this discourse were instrumental in fashioning the 'East' as a utopian alternative to Europe. Countless scholars, writers, polemicists, spiritualists, travellers and wanderers invoked Orientalist idealisations of India to critique—in the spirit of Gandhi's *Hind Swaraj*—the aggressive capitalism and territorialism of the modern West. And, as critics such as

Dennis Porter and Parminder Kaur Bakshi argue, the underground and radically dissident tradition of nineteenth-century homosexual literature drew much of its sustenance from the liberated alterity of the Orient (see Porter 1983; Bakshi 1990). Writers like E.M. Forster and Edward Carpenter, among others, imagined, wrote, thought and discovered the Orient, stereotypically, as a safeguard against the political and personal repressions of imperial Europe.

If *Orientalism* is a limited text, then it is so primarily because it fails to accommodate the possibility of difference within Oriental discourse. Sometimes, in his obdurate determination that Orientalism silenced opposition, Said, ironically, silences opposition. So also he defeats the logic of his own intellectual egalitarianism by producing and confirming a reversed stereotype: the racist Westerner. After *Orientalism*, it becomes our task not only to demonstrate the ambivalence of the Oriental stereotype, but also—and crucially—to refuse the pleasures of an Occidental stereotype. We might start to see the shape and possibility of this refusal by returning to the Orientalist archive so as to listen more carefully to the Orientalists themselves. How, for example, should we respond to William Jones, Orientalist *par excellence*, when he starts to speak vitriolically about the uncivilised cultural insularity of Europe?

> Some men have never heard of the Asiatick writings, and others will not be convinced that there is anything valuable in them; some pretend to be busy, and others are really idle; some detest the Persians, because they believe in Mahomed, and others despise their language, because they do not understand it: we all love to excuse, or to conceal, our ignorance, and are seldom willing to allow any excellence beyond the limits of our own achievements: like the savages, who thought the sun rose and set for them alone, and could not imagine that the waves, which surrounded their island, left coral and pearl upon any other shore (Jones 1991, p. 158).

Since, here we have an Orientalist critique of the exclusions which run through Western knowledges—an inversion of colonial oppositions, whereby it is the epistemological arrogance

79

of Europe which earns the charge of savagery, surely Jones' appeal on behalf of non-European knowledges exceeds the bounds of Said's book, and begs to be accommodated in a less formulaic rereading of Orientalism.

as postcolonialism's view: the critique has to come from the colonized.

Said → Marginalizing the Western culture Orientalism to critique the power of Europe.

5

Postcolonialism and feminism

In *Culture and Imperialism*, Said concedes that *Orientalism* fails to theorise adequately the resistance of the non-European world to the material and discursive onslaught of colonialism. This recent book announces its departure from Said's earlier and disablingly one-sided account of the colonial encounter: 'Never was it the case that the imperial encounter pitted an active Western intruder against a supine or inert non-Western native; there was *always* some form of active resistance and, in the overwhelming majority of cases, the resistance finally won out' (Said 1993, p. xii). However, despite this apparent recantation, Said stubbornly refuses to elevate anti-colonial *resistance* to the status of anti-colonial *critique*. The culture of resistance, he argues, finds its theoretical and political limit in the chauvinist and authoritarian boundaries of the postcolonial nation-State—itself a conformity-producing prison-house which reverses, and so merely replicates, the old colonial divisions of racial consciousness. Moreover, in its exclusively anti-Western focus, anti-colonial nationalism deflects attention away from internal orthodoxies and injustices—'the nation can become a panacea for *not* dealing with economic disparities, social injustice, and the capture of the newly independent state by a nationalist elite' (1993, p. 262). Thus, Said insists, a comprehensive dismantling of colonial hierarchies and structures needs to be matched by a reformed and imaginative reconception of colonised society and culture. It requires an enlightened intellectual consensus which 'refuses the short term blandishments of separatist and triumphalist slogans in favour of the larger, more generous human realities of community *among* cultures, peoples, and societies' (1993, p. 262). In other words, the intellectual stirrings of anti-colonialism can only be properly realised when nationalism becomes more 'critical of itself'—when it proves itself capable of directing attention 'to the abused rights of all oppressed classes' (1993, p. 264).

Said's intervention urges postcolonialism to reconsider the significance of all those other liberationist activities in the colonised world—such as those of the women's movement—which forcefully interrupt the triumphant and complacent rhetoric of the anti-colonial nation-State. 'Students of postcolonial politics', he laments, 'have not . . . looked enough at ideas that minimise orthodoxy and authoritarian or patriarchal thought, that take a severe view of the coercive nature of identity politics' (1993, p. 264). And yet, despite the force of Said's appeal, it is difficult for postcolonialism to entirely withdraw its loyalties from anti-colonial nationalism. Accordingly, it has always been troubled by the conflicting claims of nationalism and feminism. In this chapter we will focus on the discordance of race and gender within colonised cultures with a view to elucidating some of the issues surrounding the contiguities and oppositions between feminist and postcolonial theory.

Imperialist feminisms: woman (in)difference

Until recently, feminist and postcolonial theory have followed what Bill Ashcroft et al. call 'a path of convergent evolution' (Ashcroft et al., 1995, p. 249). Both bodies of thought have concerned themselves with the study and defence of marginalised 'Others' within repressive structures of domination and, in so doing, both have followed a remarkably similar theoretical trajectory. Feminist and postcolonial theory alike began with an attempt to simply invert prevailing hierarchies of gender/culture/race, and they have each progressively welcomed the poststructuralist invitation to refuse the binary oppositions upon which patriarchal/colonial authority constructs itself. It is only in the last decade or so, however, that these two parallel projects have finally come together in what is, at best, a very volatile and tenuous partnership. In a sense, the alliance between these disciplinary siblings is informed by a mutual suspicion, wherein each discourse constantly confronts its limits and exclusions in the other. In the main, there are three areas of controversy which fracture the potential unity between postcolonialism and feminism: the debate surrounding the figure of the 'third-world woman'; the problematic history of the 'feminist-as-imperialist'; and finally, the colonialist deployment of 'feminist criteria' to bolster the appeal of the 'civilising mission'.

The most significant collision and collusion of postcolonial and feminist theory occurs around the contentious figure of the 'third-world woman'. Some feminist postcolonial theorists have cogently argued that a blinkered focus on racial politics inevitably elides the 'double colonisation' of women under imperial conditions. Such theory postulates the 'third-world woman' as victim *par excellence*—the forgotten casualty of both imperial ideology, and native and foreign patriarchies. While it is now impossible to ignore the feminist challenge to the gender blindness of anti-colonial nationalism, critics such as Sara Suleri are instructive in their disavowal of the much too eager 'coalition between postcolonial and feminist theories, in which each term serves to reify the potential pietism of the other' (Suleri 1992, p. 274). The imbrication of race and gender, as Suleri goes on to argue, invests the 'third-world woman' with an iconicity which is almost 'too good to be true' (1992, p. 273).

Suleri's irascible objections to the postcolonial–feminist merger require some clarification. They need to be read as a refusal to, as it were, surrender the 'third-world woman' to the sentimental and often opportunistic enamourment with 'marginality', which—as we have seen in an earlier chapter—has come to characterise the metropolitan cult of 'oppositional criticism'. As Spivak writes, 'If there is a buzzword in cultural critique now, it is "marginality"' (Spivak 1993, p. 55). We now take it on trust that the consistent invocation of the marginal/subjugated has helped reform the aggressive canonicity of high Western culture. And yet, even as the margins thicken with political significance, there are two problems which must give pause. First, as Spivak insists, the prescription of non-Western alterity as a tonic for the ill health of Western culture heralds the perpetration of a 'new Orientalism'. Second, the metropolitan *demand* for marginality is also troublingly a *command* which consolidates and names the non-West as interminably marginal. By way of example, we might reconsider Deleuze and Guattari's celebration of 'minor' or 'deterritorialised' discourses in their influential study, *Kafka: Toward a Minor Literature* (Deleuze & Guattari 1986). These discourses or literatures, the authors inform us, inhere in 'points of nonculture or underdevelopment, linguistic Third World zones by which a language can escape, an animal enter into things, an assemblage come into play' (1986, p. 27). In Deleuze and Guattari's revolutionary manifesto, the third world becomes a stable metaphor for the 'minor' zone of nonculture and underdevelopment. Moreover, its value inheres only in its capacity to politicise or—predictably—'subvert' major, that is to say, more developed, cultural formations. Once again, then, as Gayatri Spivak suggests, the margin is at the service of the centre: 'When a cultural identity is thrust upon one because the centre wants an identifiable margin, claims for marginality assure validation from the centre' (Spivak 1993, p. 55). The 'third-world woman' is arguably housed in an 'identifiable margin'. And as critics like Suleri and Spivak insist, this accommodation is ultimately unsatisfactory.

In an impressionistic and quasi-poetic book *Woman, Native, Other*, Trinh T. Minh-ha firmly attributes the rise of the 'third-world woman' to the ideological tourism of Western/liberal feminism. Trinh's book elaborates its critique through a fictionalised—and yet all too familiar—account of the paternalistic and self-congratulatory tokenism which sustains 'Special Third World Women's' readings, workshops, meetings and seminars. In every such event, Trinh argues, the veneer of cross-cultural, sisterly colloquium disguises an unpleasant ideology of separatism. Wherever she goes, the 'native woman' is required to exhibit her ineluctable 'difference' from the primary referent of Western feminism: 'It is as if everywhere we go, we become Someone's private zoo' (Trinh 1989, p. 82). This voyeuristic craving for the colourful alterity of native women seriously compromises the seemingly egalitarian politics of liberal feminism. The consciousness of difference, identified by Trinh, sets up an implicit culturalist hierarchy wherein almost inevitably the 'native woman' suffers in contrast with her Western sibling. By claiming the dubious privilege of 'preparing the way for one's more "unfortunate" sisters', the Western feminist creates an insuperable division between 'I-who-have-made-it and You-who-cannot-make-it' (1989, p. 86). Thus, Trinh concludes, the circulation of the 'Special Third World Women's Issue', only serves to advertise the specialness of the mediating first(?) world woman.

In her influential article 'Under Western eyes: feminist scholarship and colonial discourses', Chandra Talpade Mohanty similarly discerns the play of a discursive colonialism in the 'production of the "Third World Woman" as a singular monolithic subject in some recent (Western) feminist texts' (Talpade Mohanty 1994, p. 196). Talpade Mohanty uses the term 'colonialism' very loosely to imply any relation of structural domination which relies upon a self-serving suppression of 'the heterogeneity of the subject(s) in question' (1994, p. 196). The analytic category 'third-world woman' is, thus, colonialist for two reasons—first, because its ethnocentric myopia disregards the enormous material and historical differences between 'real' third-world women; and second, because the composite 'Othering' of the 'third-world woman' becomes a self-consolidating project for Western feminism. Talpade Mohanty shows how feminists working within the social

sciences invoke the narrative of 'double colonisation' principally to contrast the political immaturity of third-world
women with the progressive ethos of Western feminism. Thus,
the representation of the average third-world woman as 'ignorant, poor, uneducated, tradition-bound, domesticated,
family-oriented, victimised', facilitates and privileges the self-
representation of Western women 'as educated, modern, as
having control over their own bodies and "sexualities", and
the "freedom" to make their own decisions' (1994, p. 200).
In other words, the implied cultural lack of the 'third-world
woman' fortifies the redemptive ideological/political plenitude
of Western feminism. To a large extent, Trinh's and Talpade
Mohanty's critiques of liberal-feminist imperialism draw upon
Said's understanding of colonial discourse as the cultural privilege of representing the subjugated Other. Both Said's
Orientalist offenders and Talpade Mohanty's feminist oppor-
tunists, seem to speak the third world through a shared
vocabulary which insists: they cannot represent themselves;
they must be represented. The 'third-world woman' can thus
be seen as yet another object of Western knowledges, simultaneously knowable and unknowing. And as Talpade Mohanty
laments, the residual traces of colonialist epistemology are all
too visible in the:

> appropriation and codification of 'scholarship' and 'knowl-
> edge' about women in the third world by particular analytic
> categories employed in writings on the subject which take as
> their primary point of reference feminist interests which have
> been articulated in the US and western Europe' (1994, p. 196).

Gayatri Spivak deserves mention here for her relentless
challenge to all those specious knowledge systems which seek
to regulate the articulation of what she calls the 'gendered
subaltern'. Although most of Spivak's scattered oeuvre touches
upon the touchy politics of knowing the Other, her early essay
'French feminism in an international frame' (1987) is exemplary in its attention to the narcissism of the liberal-feminist
investigator. In this essay, Spivak details the problematic eli-
sions which run through Julia Kristeva's *About Chinese*

Women—a text which emerged out of the sporadic French academic interest in China during the 1970s. Spivak's essay pursues Kristeva's itinerant gaze to the sun-soaked expanse of Huxian Square, where a crowd of unspeaking women picturesquely awaits the theorist's peroration. In her characteristic style, Spivak starts to interrupt Kristeva's musings and, in so doing, foregrounds the discrepancy between the visible silence of the observed Chinese women and the discursive cacophony of the observing French feminist. Spivak's exercise makes a simple point: we never *hear* the object(s) of Kristeva's investigation represent themselves. Yet, in the face of her mute native material, Kristeva abandons all scholarly decorum to hypothesise and generalise about China in terms of millennia, and always, as Spivak wryly observes, 'with no encroachment of archival evidence' (Spivak 1987, p. 137). Eventually, as Kristeva's prose starts to slip away from any reference to the verity of the onlooking gathering at Huxian Square, her fluency becomes an end in itself; a solipsistic confirmation of the investigator's discursive privilege. Indeed, as Spivak points out, the material and historical scene before Kristeva is only ever an occasion for self-elaboration:

> Her question, in the face of those silent women, is about her *own* identity rather than theirs . . . This too might be characteristic of the group of thinkers to whom I have, most generally, attached her. In spite of their occasional interest in touching the *other* of the West, of metaphysics, of capitalism, their repeated question is obsessively self-centred: if we are not what official history and philosophy say we are, who then are we (not), how are we (not)? (Spivak 1987, p. 137).

Spivak's incisive reading catches the authoritative knower in the act of 'epistemic violence'—or authoritarian knowing. *About Chinese Women* is really a book about Kristeva: a text which deploys, once again, the difference of the 'third-world woman' as grist to the mill of Western theory. Trinh's concluding remarks on the generic third-world women's seminar are relevant here: 'We did not come to hear a Third World member speak about the First(?) World, We came to listen to that voice of difference likely to bring us *what we can't have* and to divert us from the monotony of sameness' (Trinh 1989, p. 88).

The critics we have been reviewing raise significant and trenchant objections to the Western feminist investment in postcolonial matters. And yet their own critique suffers from serious limitations. Trinh, Talpade Mohanty and Spivak each idealise and essentialise the epistemological opacity of the 'real' third-world woman. By making her the bearer of meanings/experiences which are always in excess of Western analytic categories, these critics paradoxically re-invest the 'third-world woman' with the very iconicity they set out to contest. This newly reclaimed figure is now postulated as the triumphant site of anti-colonial resistance. Trinh's rampant prose valorises the racial, gendered body itself as a revolutionary archive, while Spivak, somewhat feebly, urges the academic feminist to *speak to* the subaltern woman, to learn from her repository of lived experience. If these proposals for change are somewhat suspect, it is also worth noting that each of the critics under consideration is guilty of the sort of reversed ethnocentrism which haunts Said's totalising critique of Orientalism. In refuting the composite and monolithic construction of 'native women', Spivak et al. unself-consciously homogenise the intentions of all Western feminists/feminisms. As it happens, there are always other stories tell—on both sides of the fence which separates postcolonialism from feminism.

Gendered subalterns: the (Other) woman in the attic

In its more irritable moments, then, postcolonial theory tends to regard liberal feminism as a type of neo-Orientalism. Said, we may recall, diagnoses Orientalism as a discourse which invents or orientalises the Orient for the purposes of imperial consumption: 'The Orient that appears in Orientalism, then, is a system of representations framed by a whole set of forces that brought the Orient into Western learning, Western consciousness, and later, Western empire' (Said 1991 [1978], pp. 202–3). Liberal feminism, it is argued, similarly throws in its lot with colonial knowledge systems whenever it postulates—or 'worlds'—the 'third-world woman' as a composite and monolithic category for analysis.

As Talpade Mohanty argues:

> Without the overdetermined discourse that creates the 'third world', there would be no (singular and privileged) first world. Without the 'third-world woman', the particular self-presentation of western women . . . would be problematical . . . the definition of 'the third-world woman' as a monolith might well tie into the larger economic and ideological praxis of 'disinterested' scientific inquiry and pluralism which are the surface manifestations of a latent economic and cultural colonization of the 'non-western' world (Talpade Mohanty 1994, pp. 215–16).

Thus, the axioms of imperialism are said to repeat themselves in every feminist endeavour to essentialise or prescriptively name the alterity/difference of native female Others.

The domestic quarrel between postcolonialism and feminism does not end here. If Western feminism stands convicted for its theoretical articulation of the 'third-world woman', it is also blamed for the way in which it simultaneously occludes the historical claims of this figure. To a large extent, both 'faults' inhere in the privilege of 'representation' claimed by hegemonic feminist discourses. They are two sides of the same coin. Thus, liberal academic feminism is said to silence the 'native woman' in its pious attempts to represent or speak for her. Kristeva's *About Chinese Women*, as we have seen, is a case in point. In her essay 'Can the subaltern speak?', Spivak famously elaborates some other contexts wherein contesting representational systems violently displace/silence the figure of the 'gendered subaltern'. As she writes:

> Between patriarchy and imperialism, subject-constitution and object-formation, the figure of the woman disappears, not into a pristine nothingness, but a violent shuttling which is the displaced figuration of the 'third-world woman' caught between tradition and modernisation (Spivak 1988 [1985], p. 306).

This essay argues that the 'gendered subaltern' disappears because we never hear her speak about herself. She is simply the medium through which competing discourses represent their claims; a palimpsest written over with the text of other desires, other meanings.

Spivak's earlier essay, 'Three women's texts and a critique of imperialism' (1985), offers another take on the 'disappearance' of the 'gendered subaltern' within liberal feminist discourses. Her arguments here open up a crucial area of disagreement between postcolonialism and feminism. Rather than chronicle the liberal feminist appropriation of the 'gendered subaltern', this essay queries the conspicuous absence of the 'third-world woman' within the literature which celebrates the emerging 'female subject in Europe and Anglo-America' (Spivak 1985, p. 243). Spivak argues that the high feminist norm has always been blinkered in its 'isolationist admiration' for individual female achievement. A rereading of women's history shows that the 'historical moment of feminism in the West' was itself defined 'in terms of female access to individualism' (1985, p. 246). Yet nowhere does feminist scholarship stop to consider where the battle for female individualism was played out. Nor does it concern itself with the numerous exclusions and sacrifices which might attend the triumphant achievements of a few female individuals. Spivak's essay is posed as an attempt to uncover the repressed or forgotten history of Euro-American feminism. Once again the margins reveal the mute figure of gendered subalterneity: 'As the female individualist, not quite/not male, articulates herself in shifting relationship to what is at stake, the "native female" as such (*within* discourse, *as* a signifier) is excluded from a share in this emerging norm' (1985, pp. 244–5).

Spivak furnishes her theoretical hypothesis with a sensitive and well-known critique of *Jane Eyre*. While feminist critics have conventionally read this novel as an allegorical account of female self-determination, Spivak in contrast argues that Jane Eyre's personal progress through Brontë's novel is predicated upon the violent effacement of the half-caste Bertha Mason. Bertha's function in the novel, we are told, 'is to render indeterminate the boundary between human and animal and thereby weaken her entitlement under the spirit if not the letter of the Law' (1985, p. 249). Jane gradually claims the entitlements lost by her dark double. Her rise to the licit centre of the novel, Spivak insists, requires Bertha's displacement to the fuzzy margins of narrative consciousness—it is fuelled, in this sense, by the Creole woman's literal and symbolic self-immolation.

Spivak's polemical reading of *Jane Eyre* firmly situates this cult text of Western feminism in the great age of European imperialism. The cultural and literary production of nineteenth-century Europe, she argues, is inextricable from the history and success of the imperialist project. Thus, and insofar as feminism seeks its inspirational origins in this period, it must also reconsider its historical complicity with imperialist discourses. The terms of Spivak's general challenge to feminism are elaborated in Jenny Sharpe's recent book, *Allegories of Empire* (1993). Sharpe further complicates the negotiations between feminism and postcolonialism by exhuming the difficult figure of the female imperialist, thereby exposing women's role in not only the politics but also the practice of empire. How might feminism respond to the individual achievements of this figure? Recent critics and historians have argued that the feminist battle for individual rights was considerably more successful in the colonies than 'at home'. While European civil society remained undecided as to whether women possessed the attributes and capacities of individuals, its colonial counterpart—in places like India—was considerably more amenable to the good offices of the white female subject. The imperial 'memsahib', as Rosemary Marangoly George argues, 'was a British citizen long before England's laws caught up with her' (Marangoly George 1993, p. 128). And yet she was only anchored as a full individual through her racial privileges.

The figure of the 'feminist imperialist'—much like that of the 'third-world woman'—fractures the potential unity between postcolonial and feminist scholarship. By way of example we might briefly turn to Pat Barr's early book, *The Memsahibs*. This nostalgic and eulogistic study betrays the faultlines of a narrowly 'feminist' approach to the ideologically fraught figure of the female imperialist. Barr is fierce and persuasive in her desire to reclaim the 'memsahib' from the satirical pen of male writers like Kipling and also from the apparent neglect of the masculinist archive: 'What they did and how they responded to their alien environment were seldom thought worthy of record, either by themselves or by contemporary chroniclers of the male-dominated imperial scenario' (Barr 1976, p. 1). So also and correctly Barr teaches us to read the memsahib's life in hot and dusty India as a *career*. Her favourite 'memsahib', Honoria Lawrence, makes a vocation out of good humour: 'Irritable she sometimes was, but never frivolous, nor procrastinating when it came to the duty of cheering her absent husband . . .' (1976, p. 71). Honoria's letters and diaries—enthusiastically cited by Barr—consistently professionalise the activities of wife- and mother-in-exile, housekeeper and hostess. She writes, in this vein, of the hiatus prior to her marriage and departure for India as an enervating period of unemployment: 'the unemployed energies, the unsatisfied desire for usefulness would eat me up' (1976, p. 35). Empire transforms such a life of indolence into work. The 'wives of the Lawrences and their followers', as Barr records, 'were vowed to God just as definitely as their husbands, were as closely knit in a community of work and religion' (1976, p. 103).

Barr's analysis confirms the soundness of her feminist credentials. She is ideologically pristine in the way in which she encourages her readers to appreciate the domestic labour of her heroines. And yet how might postcolonialism even begin to condone this feminist investment in imperial career opportunities. As it happens, the 'contribution' of the 'memsahib' can only be judged within the racial parameters of the imperial project. This, then, is Barr's conclusive defence of her protagonists: 'For the most part, the women loyally and stoically accepted their share of the white people's burden and lightened the weight of it with their quiet humour, their grace, and often their youth' (1976, p. 103). Not content to stop here, Barr goes on to valorise the grassroots feminism of her protagonists.

The 'angel' in the colonial home, we are told, joins the ranks of colonial missionaries to universalise the gospel of bourgeois domesticity. In the fulfilment of this endeavour she regularly turns her evangelical eye upon the glaring problem of the backward 'Indian female'. The indefatigable Annette Ackroyd braves the collective wrath of Indian patriarchy to instruct 'pupils in practical housework and to the formation of orderly and industrious habits' (Barr 1976, p. 166), while her compatriot, Flora Annie Steele, promises the Punjabi Education Board a 'primer on Hygiene for the Girls' Middle School examination to take the place of the perfectly useless Euclid' (Barr 1976, p. 160). However, whereas Barr sees only a history of self-empowerment in the figures of the well-meaning memsahibs Steele and Ackroyd, the postcolonial critic is prevented from such unreserved celebration by the recognition that these women's constitution as fully fledged 'individual subjects' is, in the end, inextricable from the hierarchies which inform the imperial project. Once again, their achievements/privileges are predicated upon the relative incivility of the untutored 'Indian female'. Meanwhile, in the wings, Spivak's 'gendered subaltern' silently awaits further instruction.

Conflicting loyalties: brothers v. sisters

In the course of its quarrel with liberal feminism, postcolonialism—as we have been arguing—fails conclusively to resolve the conflicting claims of 'feminist emancipation' and 'cultural emancipation'. It is unable to decide, as Kirsten Holst Petersen puts it, 'which is the more important, which comes first, the fight for female equality or the fight against Western cultural imperialism?' (Holst Peterson in Ashcroft et al. 1995, p. 252). These are not, of course, new questions. For if contemporary liberal feminism derives its ancestry in part from the imperialist 'memsahib', postcolonialism, no less, recuperates stubborn nationalist anxieties about the 'woman question' which typically dichotomise the claims of 'feminism' and 'anti-colonialism'. Frantz Fanon's apology for Algerian women in his book, *A Dying Colonialism* is a case in point. Fanon postulates the 'veiled Algerian woman' as a site for the playing out of colonial and anti-colonial rivalries. Accordingly, the colonial critique of Algerian patriarchy is read as a strategic attempt to fragment the unity of national revolution. The coloniser, Fanon tells us, destructures Algerian society through its women: 'If we want to destroy the structure of Algerian society, its capacity for resistance, we must first of all conquer the women; we must go and find them behind the veil where they hide themselves and in the houses where the men keep them out of sight' (Fanon 1965, pp. 57–8). Fanon's rhetoric self-consciously politicises the veil or the *haik*, thereby reconstituting colonialism as the project of 'unveiling Algeria'. Against this, nationalism appropriates the feminine *haik* as a metaphor for political elusiveness. The Algerian woman becomes a fellow revolutionary simply through her principled 'no' to the coloniser's 'reformist' invitation. She learns also to revolutionise her feminine habit: 'she goes out into the street with three grenades in her handbag or the activity report of an area in her bodice' (1965, p. 50). Fanon's appeal to the loyalties of Algerian women elaborates a characteristic nationalist anxiety which Spivak brilliantly summarises in the sentence: 'White men are saving brown women from brown men' (Spivak 1988 [1985], p. 296). Thus, in Fanon's understanding, the claims of brown compatriotism must necessarily exceed the disruptive petition of white (feminist) interlopers. The veiled Algerian woman, he confidently announces, 'in imposing such a restriction on herself, in choosing a form of existence limited in scope, was deepening her consciousness of struggle and preparing for combat' (1965, p. 66). Despite the force of Fanon's argument, interloping feminist readers may very well question his authoritative representation of Algerian womanhood and find themselves in agreement with Partha Chatterjee's recent book, *The Nation and Its Fragments*, which argues that nationalist discourse is finally 'a discourse *about* women; women do not speak here' (Chatterjee 1993b, p. 133). Seen in these terms, postcolonial theory betrays its own uneasy complicity with nationalist discourses whenever it announces itself as the only legitimate mouthpiece for native women. In another context, the publication of the American author Katherine Mayo's accusatory book, *Mother India*, in 1927 (republished in 1986) distils some further controversies surrounding the Western feminist intervention into the 'native woman question'. This sensationalist book reads, as Gandhi observed, like a drain inspector's report. Under the guise of 'disinterested inquiry', Mayo embarks on a furious invective against the unhappy condition of Indian women. In page after page she inventories the brutishness of Indian men, the horrors of child-marriage, the abjection of widowhood and, of course, the atavistic slavishness, illiteracy and unsanitary habits of Indian wives. Mayo's book, understandably, caused an uproar. Most prominent male Indian nationalists penned furious rejoinders to her allegations, and a spate of books appeared under titles like *Father India: A Reply to Mother India, A Son of Mother India Answers* and *Unhappy India.* In the face of Mayo's assessment of Indians as unfit for self-rule—on account of their heinous attitudes toward women—sane critics like Gandhi and Tagore, calmly dismissed the book as another tired apology for the colonial civilising mission. Other more traumatised critics, in their anti-feminist vitriol, betrayed troubling aspects of the nationalist possessiveness about 'native women'.

The anonymous but indisputably male author of the hysterical *Sister India*, for example, insists that Mayo's feminist criterion are simply foreign to India. He invokes the rhetoric of cultural authenticity to argue that the emancipation of Indian women must be couched in an indigenous idiom. Mayo's recommendations are flawed primarily because they invite Indian women to become poor copies of their Western counterparts:

> It would be an evil day for India if Indian women indiscriminately copy and imitate Western women. Our women will progress in their own way . . . We are by no means prepared to think that the Western woman of today is a model to be copied. What has often been termed in the West as the

emancipation of women is only a glorified name for the disintegration of the family ('World Citizen' 1927, p. 163).

Not only does *Sister India* demonise Western feminism, it also reveals the extent to which the nation authenticates its distinct cultural identity through its women. Partha Chatterjee's work on Indian anti-colonial nationalism is instructive here—drawing attention to the subtle nuances of the nationalist compromise with the invasive hegemony of colonial/Western values. Indian nationalists, he argues, dealt with the compulsive claims of Western civilisation by dividing the domain of culture into two discrete spheres—the material and the spiritual. It was hard to contest the superiority and domination of the West in the *material* sphere. But on the other hand, as texts like Gandhi's *Hind Swaraj* proclaimed, no cultural rival could possibly match the superiority of India's *spiritual* essence. Thus, as Chatterjee writes, while it was deemed necessary to cultivate and imitate the material accomplishments of Western civilisation, it was compulsory to simultaneously preserve and police the spiritual properties of national culture. And in the catalogue of the nation's spiritual effects, the home and its keeper acquired a troublesome preeminence. In Chatterjee's words: 'The home in its essence must remain unaffected by the profane activities of the material world—and woman is its representation' (Chatterjee 1993b, p. 120).

This, then, is the context for the nationalist trepidation about the 'Westernisation' of Indian women. The irate author of *Sister India* takes his cue from nationalist discourse in his anxiety that Mayo's book might urge the custodians of national (spiritual) domesticity to bring Europe imitatively into the foundational home. Chatterjee's sources reveal that the nationalist investment in 'authentic' Indian womanhood resulted in the nomination of a new enemy—the hapless 'memsahib'. As he writes:

> To ridicule the idea of a Bengali woman trying to imitate the ways of a *memsaheb* . . . was a sure recipe calculated to evoke raucous laughter and moral condemnation in both male and

female audiences . . . What made the ridicule stronger was the constant suggestion that the Westernised woman was fond of useless luxury and cared little for the well-being of the home (1993b, p. 122).

Thus, in order to establish the necessary *difference* between Indian and Western women, (male) nationalism systematically demonised the 'memsahib'—as a particularly ugly passage about Katherine Mayo from *Sister India* exemplifies: 'She is an old maid of 49, and has all along, been absorbed in the attempt to understand the mystery of sex. If she were a married lady, she would have easily understood what the mystery was . . . As soon as she gets married, she will be an improved girl, and an improved woman' ('World Citizen' 1927, pp. 103–4).

In this account of nationalist anxieties about Western 'feminism' we can discern the historical origins of the postcolonial animosity toward liberal feminism. Equally, it is important to note that the traumatic nationalist negotiation of the 'woman question' establishes a direct and problematic enmity between 'brown men' and 'white women'. No one has understood or articulated this historical hostility more eloquently than E. M. Forster in his *A Passage To India*. The native men of Forster's Chandrapore despise the memsahibs. 'Granted the exceptions', as Forster's Aziz agrees, 'all Englishwomen are haughty and venal' (Forster 1979, p. 33). This disdain is, of course, amply reciprocated, and as Mrs Callendar, the wife of the local civil surgeon, observes: 'the best thing one can do to a native is to let him die' (1979, p. 44). Forster's fictional counterpart, Fielding, accurately diagnoses the implacable hostility between 'memsahibs' and 'native men': 'He had discovered that it is possible to keep in with Indians and Englishmen, but that he who would also keep in with Englishwomen must drop the Indians. The two wouldn't combine' (1979, p. 74). These tensions, announced from the very beginning of the novel, famously explode in the Marabar Caves incident. From this point onward, the superior race clusters around the inferior sex, while the inferior race announces its allegiance to the superior sex. Between the female victim, Adela Quested, and the colonised underdog, Dr Aziz, the choices are, indeed, very stark. The choices between the obnoxious Katherine Mayo and the awful author of *Sister India* are starker still. Yet this is, surely, a very old quarrel and it is possible for postcolonialism and feminism to exceed the limits of their respective histories.

Between men: rethinking the colonial encounter

A productive area of collaboration between postcolonialism and feminism presents itself in the possibility of a combined offensive against the aggressive myth of both imperial and nationalist masculinity. In the last few years, a small but significant group of critics has attempted to reread the colonial encounter in these terms as a struggle between competing masculinities. We have already seen how colonial and colonised women are postulated as the symbolic mediators of this (male) contestation. If anti-colonial nationalism authenticated itself through female custodians of spiritual domesticity, the male imperial ethic similarly distilled its 'mission' through the figure of the angel in the colonial home. Anne McClintock's recent book, *Imperial Leather*, points to some aspects of the empire's investment in its women. As she writes: 'Controlling women's sexuality, exalting maternity and breeding a virile race of empire-builders was widely perceived as the paramount means for controlling the health and wealth of the male imperial body' (McClintock 1995, p. 47). Other writers have also drawn attention to ways in which the colonial civilising mission represented itself through the self-sacrificing, virtuous and domesticated figure of the 'white' housewife. The figure of woman, Jenny Sharpe argues, was 'instrumental in shifting a colonial system of meaning from self-interest and moral superiority to self-sacrifice and racial superiority' (1993, p. 7).

In this context, McClintock usefully foregrounds the hidden aspect of sexual rivalry which accompanied the restitution and reinvention of imperial/anti-colonial 'manliness' and patriarchy. She argues that the masculinity of empire was articulated, in the first instance, through the symbolic feminisation of conquered geographies, and in the erotic economy of colonial 'discovery' narratives. Vespucci's mythic disclosure of the virginal American landscape is a case in point: 'Invested with the male prerogative of naming, Vespucci renders America's identity a dependent extension of his, and stakes male Europe's territorial rights to her body and, by extension, the fruits of her land' (1995, p. 26). In another context, Fanon shows how this threat of territorial/sexual dispossession produces, in the colonised male, a reciprocal fantasy of sexual/territorial repossession: 'I marry white culture, white beauty, white whiteness. When my restless hands caress those white breasts, they grasp white civilisation and dignity and make them mine' (Fanon 1967, p. 63). Needless to say, these competing desires find utterance in competing anxieties. Sharpe's work suggests that the discourse of rape surrounding English women in colonial India positions Englishmen as their avengers, thereby permitting violent 'strategies of counterinsurgency to be recorded as the restoration of moral order' (Sharpe 1993, p. 6). Correspondingly, Fanon insists that the 'aura' of rape surrounding the veiled Algerian woman provokes the 'native's bristling resistance' (Fanon 1967, p. 47).

Fanon's exploration, in *Black Skin, White Masks*, of the sexual economy underpinning the colonial encounter in Algeria leads him to conclude that the colonised black man is the 'real' Other for the colonising white man. Several critics and historians have extended this analysis to the Indian context to argue that colonial masculinity defined itself with reference to the alleged effeminacy of Indian men. The infamous Thomas Macaulay, among others, gives full expression to this British disdain for the Indian apology for maleness:

> The physical organisation of the Bengali is feeble even to effeminacy. He live[s] in a constant vapour bath. His pursuits are sedentary, his limbs delicate, his movements languid. During many ages he has been trampled upon by men of bolder and hardy deeds. Courage, independence, veracity, are qualities to which his constitution and his situation are equally unfavourable (cited in Rosselli 1980, p. 122).

99

In other words, India is colonisable because it lacks real men. Macaulay's description fully illustrates what Ashis Nandy describes as the colonial homology between sexual and political dominance. By insisting upon the racial effeminacy of the Bengali (not quite) male, Macaulay reformulates the colonial relationship in terms of the 'natural' ascendancy of men over women. Accordingly, he renders as hyper-masculine the unquestioned dominance of European men at home and abroad. As Nandy writes:

> Colonialism, too, was congruent with the existing Western sexual stereotypes and the philosophy of life which they represented. It produced a cultural consensus in which political and socio-economic dominance symbolised the dominance of men and masculinity over women and femininity (Nandy 1983, p. 4).

The discourse of colonial masculinity was thoroughly internalised by wide sections of the nationalist movement. Some nationalists responded by lamenting their own emasculation, others by protesting it. Historians have drawn attention, in this regard, to the reactive resurgence of physical and, relatedly, militaristic culture within the Indian national movement.

Ashis Nandy elides the story of Indian nationalism's derivative masculinity to tell an altogether different—and considerably more interesting—story about dissident androgyny. *The Intimate Enemy* (1983) theorises the emergence of a protest against the colonial cult of masculinity, both within the Indian national movement and also on the fringes of nineteenth-century British society. Nandy's analysis reclaims diverse figures like Gandhi and Oscar Wilde. Gandhi, as Nandy shows us, repudiated the nationalist appeal to maleness on two fronts—first, through his systematic critique of male sexuality; and second, through his self-conscious aspiration for bisexuality or the desire, as he put it, to become 'God's eunuch' (see Mehta 1977, p. 194). Gandhi's radical self-fashioning gives 'femaleness' an equal share in the making of anti-colonial subjectivity. So also, by refusing to partake in the disabling logic of colonial sexual binaries, he successfully complicates the authoritative signature of colonial masculinity. From the other side, Wilde similarly protests the dubious worth of manly British robustness. As with Gandhi, his critique of conventional sexual identities and sexual norms threatens what Nandy describes as 'a basic postulate of the colonial attitude in Britain' (Nandy 1983, p. 44). There are countless other examples—Edward Carpenter, Lytton Strachey and Virginia Woolf are all, as Nandy writes, 'living protests against the world view associated with colonialism' (1983, p. 43). Postcolonialism and feminism own a potential meeting ground in these figures—in Carpenter's thesis about the 'intermediate sex' and in Woolf's contentious delineation of androgyny. And perhaps there is some hope of a cross-cultural and inter-theoretical accord in Woolf's passionate and feminist critique of bellicose colonial masculinity in *Three Guineas*:

> We can still shake out eggs from newspapers; still smell a peculiar and unmistakable odour in the region of Whitehall and Westminister. And abroad the monster has come more openly to the surface. There is no mistaking him there. He has widened his scope. He is interfering now with your liberty; he is dictating how you shall live; he is making distinctions not merely between sexes, but between the races. You are feeling in your own persons what your mothers felt when they were shut out, when they were shut up, because you are Jews, because you are democrats, because of race, because of religion (Woolf [1938] reprinted 1992, p. 304).

Much like Wilde and Gandhi, Woolf's denunciation of aggressive masculinity supplies the basis of a shared critique of chauvinist national and colonial culture. While some critics have fruitfully explored the terms of such a critique, its full potential awaits theoretical elaboration.

6

Imagining community: the question of nationalism

As we have seen, the encounter with feminism urges postcolonialism to produce a more critical and self-reflexive account of cultural nationalism. In this chapter, we will consider some grounds for a postcolonial defence of the anti-colonial nation. It is generally acknowledged—even by the most 'cosmopolitan' postcolonial critics—that nationalism has been an important feature of decolonisation struggles in the third world. Thus, for all his reservations about cultural particularism, Said concedes that:

> Along with armed resistance in places as diverse as nineteenth-century Algeria, Ireland and Indonesia, there also went considerable efforts in cultural resistance almost everywhere, the assertions of nationalist identities, and, in the political realm, the creation of associations and parties whose common goal was self-determination and national independence (Said 1993, p. xii).

Accordingly, postcolonial critics recognise that any adequate account of the colonial encounter requires a theoretical and historical engagement with the issue of Asian and African nationalisms. And in this regard, a number of questions present themselves: are these insurgent nationalisms purely or simply reactions against the fact of colonial dominance? Is the idea of the 'nation' germane to the cultural topography of the third world, or is anti-colonial nationalism a foreign and 'derivative' discourse? And, finally, is it possible to reconcile the often-aggressive particularism of Asian and African nation-States with the late twentieth century dream of internationalism and globalisation?

Good and bad nationalisms

In seeking to negotiate the complex implications arising from 'the nationalism question', postcolonial studies is forced to make an intervention into a vexed discourse. So while Benedict Anderson famously argues that 'nation-ness is the most universally legitimate value in the political life of our times' (Anderson 1991, p. 3), at the same time, and paradoxically, competing or 'separatist' appeals for nationhood are generally regarded as symptoms of political illegitimacy. It would appear, then, that while some nations are 'good' and progressive, others are 'bad' and reactionary. In his illuminating essay, 'Nationalisms against the State', David Lloyd attributes the persistence of this chronic distinction between 'good' and 'bad', or 'legitimate' and 'illegitimate', nationalisms to a deeper contradiction that has always occupied the troubled heart of the discourses surrounding nationalism (Lloyd 1993a). The selective and current bias of Western anti-nationalism, he maintains, emerges out of a historically deep-seated metropolitan antipathy toward anti-colonial movements in the third world. Thus—in response to the threat of decolonisation movements—liberalism has been unable to adjudicate between, on the one hand, the world historical claims of Western nationalism, and, on the other, the specifically anti-Western and oppositional development of cultural nationalism in the 'third world'. Western anti-nationalism, Lloyd suggests, has a history in imperialist thought which postcolonialism cannot afford to ignore. What, then, are the conditions under which nationalism

103

has obtained the theoretical endorsement, and hostility, of Western scholars and critics?

For many theorists, the unquestionable legitimacy of nationalism accrues from its labour on behalf of modernity. Writers like Ernst Gellner and Benedict Anderson, in particular, defend nationalism as the only form of political organisation which is appropriate to the social and intellectual condition of the modern world. Gellner attributes the emergence of nationalism to the epochal 'shift' from pre-industrial to industrial economies, and argues that, as forms of social organisation become more complex and intricate they come to require a more homogenous and cooperative workforce and polity. Thus, industrial society produces the economic conditions for national consciousness—which it consolidates politically through the supervisory agency of the nation-State. In Gellner's words:

> . . . mobility, communication, size due to refinement of specialisation—imposed by the industrial order by its thirst for affluence and growth, obliges its social units to be large and yet culturally homogenous. The maintenance of this kind of inescapable high (because literate) culture requires protection from a state . . . (Gellner 1983, p. 141).

In a similar vein, Anderson argues that the birth of nationalism in Western Europe is coeval with the dwindling—if not the death—of religious modes of thought. The rationalist secularism of the Enlightenment brings with it the devastation of old systems of belief and sociality embedded in the chimeral mysteries of divine kingship, religious community, sacred languages and cosmological consciousness. Nationalism, Anderson tells us, fills up the existential void left in the wake of paradise: 'What was then required was a secular transformation of fatality into continuity, contingency into meaning . . . few things were (are) better suited to this end than an idea of the nation' (Anderson 1991, p. 11). The nation, then, is the product of a radically secular and modern imagination, invoked through the cultural forms of the novel and newspaper in the godless expanse of what Anderson calls 'homogenous empty time'.

Gellner's and Anderson's accounts of the teleological necessity—indeed, inevitability—of the modern nation-State reveal a Hegelian bias. As is well known, Hegel posits the story of 'mankind' as the story of our progression from the darkness of nature into the light of 'History'. The prose of 'History', in turn, delivers the narrative of modernity. 'History' is the vehicle of rational self-consciousness through which the incomplete human spirit progressively acquires an improved sense of its own totality. In other words, 'History' generates the rational process through which the alienated essence of the individual citizen acquires a cohesive and reparative identity in the common life of the nation. Thus, for Hegel, the overlapping narratives of 'Reason', 'Modernity' and 'History' reveal their proper 'end'—the final truth of their significance—in the consolidated form of the nation-State (see Hegel 1975).

Hegel's monumental and influential defence of civil society furnishes the ideology of nation-ness and, concomitantly, points to the process through which the nation-State has been rendered as the most canonical form of political organisation and identity in the contemporary world. In these post-Hegelian times, 'productive' international conversations and transactions can only be conducted between nations and their real or potential representatives. So, also, individual subjectivity is most readily and conveniently spoken through the idiom of citizenship. And yet—to return to an earlier point in this discussion—despite general assumptions about the universal desirability of nation-ness, how is it that liberal thinkers remain hostile to the growing cacophony of national desires in some parts of Asia, Africa, and Central and Eastern Europe? Why is it so widely acknowledged that these 'new' nationalisms are retrogressive, narcissistic, transgressive, uncontainable?

In answer to some of these questions, Lloyd directs attention to a fundamental ambivalence which marks even the most enthusiastic (Western) celebrations of 'progressive' nationalism. In the same works which highlight its irreducible modernity, nationalism is also, and paradoxically, postulated as the catalyst for 'pre-modern' or 'atavistic' sentiments (Lloyd 1993a). While it is acknowledged that the historical momentum toward the nation-State fulfils the Hegelian expectation of a successively expansive and rational civil society, writers such as Gellner and Anderson concede that the poetics of 'national belonging' are often underscored by 'irrational', 'superstitious' and 'folkloric' beliefs or practices. How else can we explain the alacrity with which citizens are willing both to kill and to die for their nations?

Tom Nairn's work offers an instructive response to the self-doubt which troubles most liberal engagements with nationalist discourse. It is Nairn's contention that the genetic code of *all* nationalisms is simultaneously inscribed by the contradictory signals of what he calls 'health' and 'morbidity': 'forms of "irrationality" (prejudice, sentimentality, collective egoism, aggression etc.) stain the lot of them' (Nairn 1977, pp. 347–8). If the rhetoric of national development secures a forward-looking vision, the corresponding—and equally powerful—rhetoric of national attachment invokes the latent energies of custom and tradition. Thus, nationalism, figured like the two-faced Roman god Janus, or like Walter Benjamin's 'Angel of History', is riven by the paradox that it encourages societies to:

> propel themselves forward to a certain sort of goal (industrialisation, prosperity, equality with other peoples etc.) *by a certain sort of regression*—by looking inwards, drawing more deeply upon their indigenous resources, resurrecting past folk-heroes and myths about themselves and so on (Nairn 1977, p. 348).

Notably, however, rather than simply condemning the atavistic underpinnings of nationalism, Nairn reads the nostalgic yearnings of nationhood as *compensatory*—as an attempt to mitigate the onerous burden of 'progress': 'Thus does nationalism stand over the passage to modernity, for human society. As human kind is forced through its strait doorway, it must look desperately back into the past, to gather strength wherever it can be found for the ordeal of development' (1977, p. 348–9).

Nairn's analysis offers a vital understanding of nationalism's structural vulnerability—of its intrinsically unstable, self-deconstructing discourse. While embodying the idea of universal progress and modernity characteristic of the European Enlightenment, nationalism—it would appear—also incorporates the conditions for an internal critique of its own foundational modernity. It is thus both 'good' and 'bad', both normalising and rebellious:

> . . . the substance of national*ism* as such is always morally, politically, humanly ambiguous. This is why moralising perspectives on the phenomenon always fail, whether they praise or berate it. They will simply seize on one face or another of the creature, and will not admit there is a common head conjoining them (1977, p. 348).

Of course, as Nairn recognises, the ideology of modernity is unlikely to concede the dangerous hybridity of its favourite child. And it is at this point in his argument that we can begin to formulate a postcolonial understanding of the impulse underpinning Western anti-nationalism. In the light of Nairn's analysis, could we, for instance, diagnose metropolitan anti-nationalism as an attempt to purge European nationalism of its own atavism, and in so doing, to project 'regressive' nationalisms elsewhere? Indeed, much Western anti-nationalism is informed by the assumption that the progressive history of the nation swerves dangerously off course in its anti-colonial manifestation, and that relatedly cultural nationalism tragically distorts the foundational modernity of nation-ness. Eric Hobsbawm's reflections on contemporary nationalisms argue just such a case:

> . . . the characteristic nationalist movements of the late twentieth century are essentially negative, or rather divisive . . . [They are mostly] rejections of modern modes of political organisation, both national and supranational. Time and again they seem to be reactions of weakness and fear, attempts to

erect barricades to keep at bay the forces of the modern world (Hobsbawm 1990; cited in Lloyd 1993a, p. 2).

Hobsbawm's critique of inaccurate or deluded late twentieth century nationalisms is chronologically inclusive of anti-colonial struggles in Asia and Africa. And in this regard, his insistence on the erroneously anti-modern nature of these insurgent nationalisms carries within it the echo of an earlier Hegelian perception of the 'lack' characterising the ancient cultures of the 'East'. Hegel's philosophy of history notoriously conveys the notion that civilisation (and modernity) travels West. In this scheme of things, the non-West is consigned to the nebulous prehistory of civilisation and, thereby, of the completed and proper nation-State. Thus, nationalism outside the West can only ever be premature and partial—a threat to the enlightened principles of the liberal state and, thereby, symptomatic of a failed or 'incomplete' modernity (see Hegel 1910; Butler 1977, pp. 40–64).

Nothing in the preceding discussion is meant to condone the horrific violence justified in the name of nationalism. East or West, we are now aware of the xenophobia, racism and loathing which attends the rhetoric of particularism. Nationalism has become the popular pretext for contemporary disquisitions of intolerance, separating Croatians and Serbians, Greeks and Macedonians, Estonians and Russians, Slovaks and Czechs, Armenians and Azerbaijanis, Israelis and Palestinians, Hindus and Muslims. And while we have been focussing primarily on the Western/liberal squeamishness about non-Western nationalisms, some of the most compelling recent critiques of nationalist ideology have emerged out of distinctly postcolonial quarters. In particular—as we have seen—Said's *Culture and Imperialism* stands out for its relentless disavowal of the 'third world's' post-imperial regression into combative and dissonant forms of nativism.

It is Said's contention that in their desperate assertions of civilisational alterity, postcolonial nations submit all too easily to a defiant and puerile rejection of imperial cultures. The result is a form of reactionary politics, whose will-to-difference is articulated through the procedures of what Nietzche has called *ressentiment* and Adorno, after him, theorised as 'negative dialectics'. In other words, enterprises such as Senghor's *négritude*, the Rastafarian movement, Hindu nationalism and Yeats' occultism are each, according to Said, limited by an essentially 'negative' and defensive apprehension of their own society and, relatedly, of 'civilised' European modernity (Said 1993, p. 275). For Said, this project is ultimately self-defeating as it merely reiterates the binary oppositions and hierarchies of colonial discourse. Thus, Yeats' mysticism, his nostalgic revival of Celtic myths, his recalcitrant fantasies of old Ireland are already underscored by the jaundiced colonial cognition of Irish backwardness and racial difference. To accept nativism, in other words:

> . . . is to accept the consequences of imperialism, the racial, religious, and political divisions imposed by imperialism itself. To leave the historical world for the metaphysics of essences like *négritude*, Irishness, Islam or Catholicism is to abandon history for essentialisations that have the power to turn human beings against each other' (Said 1993, p. 276).

Said's irate critique of overheated nativism is predicated upon his own overarching cosmopolitanism. He holds the view that nationalism—especially in its anti-colonial manifestation—is both a necessary and now entirely obsolete evil. If nationalism fuels the oppositional energies of decolonisation struggles, the accomplishment of postcolonial independence should sound the death knoll for fanatical nation-making. History requires the graceful withering away of all nation-States. However, while this vision may be, in itself, pre-eminently desirable, Said's argument is inclined to capitulate to the liberal perception of anti-colonial 'nativism' as the only remaining obstacle to the democratic utopia of free and fair internationalism. A more just analysis demands that we first reconsider the discursive conditions which colour the somewhat paranoid antipathy toward the bogey of 'nativism'.

In this context, we need to pay renewed attention to Seamus Deane's claim that insofar as colonial and imperial nations *characteristically* universalise themselves, 'they regard any insurgency against them as necessarily provincial' (Deane 1990, p. 9). While anti-colonial insurgency may very often, as Said points out, seek its deliverance in a defiant provincialism, it is equally true that the charge of 'nativism' is all too readily invoked to pronounce the illegitimacy of insurgency. Nativism or atavism constitute, as we have seen, the indispensable and convenient Other to the arrogant discourse of modernity. This deceptively neat opposition between positive or modern and negative or non-modern nationalisms renders all local, plural and recalcitrant varieties of nationalism as inevitably inadequate and subordinate. Lloyd's comments on Irish national movements are, once again, startlingly apposite:

> In the writings of nationalism we can observe, as it were, the anxieties of canon formation, since negation largely takes place through the judgement that a given cultural form is either too marginal to be representative or, in terms that recapitulate those of imperialism itself, a primitive manifestation in need of development or cultivation (Lloyd 1993b, p. 5).

Furthermore, it is important to recognise that forms of nationalism which refuse the singular content of modernity are not necessarily all designed to turn human beings against each other. Mercifully there is still a world of difference between Yeats' occultism and the Taliban militia's fanatical edict against female literacy in wartorn Afghanistan. And modernity itself, far from being simply a benefit, can also be read, as Nairn reasons, as an 'ordeal', which demands the palliative energies of so-called 'atavistic' enterprises.

Midnight's children: the politics of nationhood

From another perspective, the postcolonial attachment to nationalism is informed by the historical apprehension that the condition of Asian and African 'postcoloniality' has been mediated and accomplished through the discourses and structures of nation-ness. Thus, the project of *becoming* postcolonial—of arriving into a decisive moment after colonialism—has usually been commemorated and legitimated through the foundation of independent nation-states. So, also, nationalism has supplied the revolutionary vocabulary for various decolonisation struggles, and it has long been acknowledged as the political vector through which disparate anti-colonial movements acquire a cohesive revolutionary shape and form. Or, to put this differently, through its focus on a common enemy, nationalism elicits and integrates the randomly distributed energies of miscellaneous popular movements. Thus, for example, Indian nationalism, as Ranajit Guha writes, achieves its entitlement through the systematic mobilisation, regulation, disciplining and harnessing of 'subaltern' energy (Guha 1992).

In another context, Fanon similarly foregrounds nationalism's capacity to distil a shared experience of dominance. Nationalism, Fanon argues, responds to the violence of colonialism by augmenting a vertical solidarity between the peasantry, workers, capitalists, feudal landowners and the bourgeoisie elite. Moreover, this consolidated counteroffensive serves another end—it revolutionises the most retrograde and moribund aspects of the colonised society: 'This people that has lost its birthright, that is used to living in the narrow circle of feuds and rivalries, will now proceed in an atmosphere of solemnity to cleanse and purify the face of the nation as it appears in the various localities' (Fanon 1990, p. 105).

Although Fanon's writings maintain a deep ambivalence toward the political desirability of an entrenched and centralised postcolonial nation-State, he remains unequivocally committed to the therapeutic necessity of anti-colonial national agitation. While nationalism comes under suspicion as the only legitimate end of decolonisation, it is nevertheless postulated as the principal remedial means whereby the colonised culture overcomes the psychological damage of colonial racism. Thus, in *The Wretched of the Earth* Fanon privileges nationalism for its capacity to heal the historical wounds inflicted by the 'Manichean' structure of colonial culture which confines the colonised to a liminal, barely human existence. In this context,

111

nationalism responds to the urgent task of rehumanisation, of regaining an Edenic wholeness. It becomes a process of reterritorialisation and repossession which replaces the 'twofold citizenship' of colonial culture with a radically unified counter-culture. By challenging the fallacious racial priority of the coloniser, the native, Fanon tells us, discovers the courageous idiom of equality: 'For if, in fact, my life is worth as much as the settler's, his glance no longer shrivels me up nor freezes me, and his voice no longer turns me into stone. I am no longer on tenterhooks in his presence; in fact, I don't give a damn for him' (Fanon 1990, p. 35). In his extensive writings on *swaraj*—or self-rule—in India, Gandhi defends the nationalist project in similar terms for its incitement to *abhaya*, or fearlessness. So also, Ngugi, Cabral and Mboya, among others, have variously extolled the recuperative benefits of anti-colonial nationalisms within Africa.

Writers like Benita Parry add a further dimension to the defence of anti-colonial nationalism by arguing that the memory of anti-colonial nationalisms in Asia and Africa might help to politicise the abstract discursivity of some postcolonial theory. Parry maintains that the ideologically correct censuring of 'nativist' resistance is tantamount to a rewriting of the anti-colonial archive. Given its poststructuralist inheritance, recent postcolonial critique tends to favour those varieties of counter-hegemonic anti-colonialisms which subvert rather than reverse the chronic oppositions of colonial discourse. This theoretical bias—fully developed in some of Homi Bhabha's work—seeks evidence for the dispersed and dislocated subjectivity of the colonised which, we are told, defies containment within colonialism's ideological apparatus. Within this reasoning, the native insurgent is shown to confound the logic of colonial domination through a refusal to occupy his/her designated subject position within colonialism's discursive cartography. In fact, for a writer like Bhabha, the slippery colonised subject is intrinsically unassimilable within the ideological boundaries of Fanon's Manichean colonial city. Without discounting the transgressive availability of such polysemic anti-colonial subjectivities, in deference to a sense of *realpolitik*

112

we still need to listen carefully to, for example, Fanon's categorical delineation of a situated, monolithic and combative national identity. And, as Parry argues, in order to do justice to the politics elaborated by anti-colonial revolutionaries like Fanon, 'it is surely necessary to refrain from a sanctimonious reproof of modes of writing resistance which do not conform to contemporary theoretical rules about discursive radicalism' (Parry 1994, p. 179). It may well be true that nativism fails ultimately to divest itself of the hierarchical divisions which inform the colonial relationship. Nevertheless, anti-colonial counter-narratives, as Parry insists:

> did challenge, subvert and undermine the ruling ideologies, and nowhere more so than in overthrowing the hierarchy of coloniser/colonised, the speech and stance of the colonised refusing a position of subjugation and dispensing with the terms of the coloniser's definitions (1994, p. 176).

Even if nationalism is theoretically 'outmoded', it still constitutes the—albeit forgotten—revolutionary archive of contemporary postcoloniality.

A derivative discourse?

The energies of the anti-colonial nationalisms under review are, as we have seen, fuelled by an indomitable will-to-difference. In its intensely recuperative mode, national consciousness refuses the universalising geography of empire, and names its insurgent cultural alterity through the nation—as 'Indian', 'Kenyan', 'Algerian' etcetera. And yet herein lies the paradox at the heart of anti-colonial nationalism. It is generally agreed that nation-ness and nationalism are European inventions which came into existence toward the end of the eighteenth century. Anderson, among others, persuasively argues that this newly contrived European nation-ness immediately acquired a 'modular' character which rendered it capable of dissemination and transplantation in a variety of disparate terrains. In his words, 'The "nation" proved an invention on which it was impossible to secure a patent. It became available for pirating

113

by widely different, and sometimes unexpected, hands' (Anderson 1991, p. 67).

By consigning all subsequent nationalisms to a typology of 'piracy', Anderson refuses to recognise the possibility of alternative, variant and *different* nationalisms. In this reading all 'post-European' nationalisms are altogether divested of creativity. They are, at best, surreptitious and vaguely unlawful enterprises posing or masquerading as the real thing.

Of course, Anderson's pessimistic insistence on the homogeneity of all nationalisms can be seen as severely limited and open to contestation. Nevertheless, as Partha Chatterjee's sensitive reading of anti-colonial nationalisms reveals, the terms of Anderson's analysis do vitiate the imagining of nation-ness in colonies like India (Chatterjee 1993a). And so it is that the project of Indian nation-making is plagued by anxieties of imitativeness, by the apprehension that Indian nationalism is just a poor copy or derivation of European post-Enlightenment discourse.

There is a general consensus among liberal historians that the formative lessons of nationalism were literally acquired in the colonial classroom through the teaching and transmission of European national histories. Anderson contends that the vast network of colonial educational apparatuses variously enabled Vietnamese children to absorb the revolutionary thought of Enlightenment *philosophes*, Indian children to co-opt the principles of the Magna Carta and the Glorious Revolution, and Congolese children to discover the energies which underscored Belgium's independence struggle against Holland (Anderson 1991, p. 118). In a similar vein the historian Percival Spear claims the achievements of Indian nationalism for Europe. In an account which reads very much like Anderson's description of the secular 'dawn' of European nationalism, Spear maintains that Westernisation/modernity forges its way through the mist of pre-modern religiosity, replacing old gods with the new sentiments of nationalism (Spear 1990, p. 166). In this way, then, the literature of the rulers hoists itself on its own petard by communicating to its subject audience the values of civil liberties and constitutional self-government. No one, Spear tells us, 'could be in contact with Englishmen at that time for long or read Shakespeare (prescribed reading in the colleges) without catching the infection of nationalism' (1990, p. 166). Spear's historiography corroborates the view that anti-colonial nationalism remains trapped within the structures of thought from which it seeks to differentiate itself—that, in short, it takes Europe to invent the language of decolonisation. So, also, Anderson claims that:

> The nineteenth-century colonial state . . . dialectically engendered the grammar of the nationalisms that eventually arose to combat it. Indeed one might go so far as to say that the state imagined its local adversaries, as in an ominous prophetic dream, well before they came into existence (Anderson 1991, p. xiv).

Plagued by such anxieties of derivativeness, anti-colonial nationalists were doubly troubled by the knowledge that colonialism was itself a type of nationalism. In other words, the problem was not just that the lessons of anti-colonial nationalisms were taught paradoxically by the (colonial) oppressor, but rather that the rapacious territorial energies of nineteenth-century colonialism were themselves fuelled by the ideology of nineteenth-century nationalism. Imperialism, as earlier writers in the Marxist tradition were well aware, is simply the aggressive face of European nationalism. After postcolonialism, the idea of imperialism has almost exclusively come to imply the processes and consequences which accompanied the historical domination of the 'third world' by the 'first', with the 'third world' designated as the proper object of imperialist histories. Thus, most recent studies of 'imperialism' tend to foreground its impact upon the economy, culture and politics of formerly imperialised nations. Yet, writers such as Lenin, Bukharin and Hilferding understood imperialism not as the relationship between coloniser and colony, but rather as a relationship of antagonism and rivalry between the ruling elite in competitive European nation-States (see Brewer 1980; Jameson 1990). The consequent scramble for markets and territories resulted in what Anderson calls the birth of 'official nationalism'—an

115

enterprise which combined dynasticism and nation-ness to expand or stretch 'the short, tight skin of the nation over the gigantic body of the empire' (Anderson 1991, p. 86). On a similar note, David Cannadine's detailed study, 'The British Monarchy, c. 1820–1977' (Cannadine 1983), suggests that the rituals of monarchism were reinvented between 1877 and 1914 in order to produce self-consciously the British nation as empire. Similar trends in Germany, Austria and Russia deployed the rhetoric of dynastic aggrandisement to instantiate the symbiosis of nationalism and imperialism (Cannadine 1983, p. 121). In this regard, the crisis of imitativeness within anti-colonial nationalism assumes existential proportions. For its problem is not simply, as Chatterjee puts it, to produce 'a different discourse, yet one that is dominated by another' (Chatterjee 1993a, p. 42), rather it has to consider that, 'it is, *mutatis mutandis*, a copy of that by which it felt itself to be oppressed' (Deane 1990, p. 8).

In this regard, we need also to recognise that if nationalism permeates the expansionist politics of empire, it is equally constitutive of imperialist ideology, of the logic which compounds the crude rhetoric of *la mission civilisatrice*. This point is compellingly elucidated in Tzvetan Todorov's monumental analysis of Enlightenment thought (Todorov 1993). Todorov discerns the incipience of colonial thinking in the debate between nationalism and cosmopolitanism which obsessed thinkers as diverse as Montesquieu, Cloots and Maurras. Montesquieu famously retained an exemplary and clear commitment to the ethics of an *esprit général*, whereby the claims of the 'citizen' were to remain secondary to those of the 'man', and those of the world were automatically to supersede those of the nation.

Other lesser thinkers resolved the conflict between home and the world through an insidiously Kantian sleight of hand: the interests of a particular country were defensible insofar as these interests were universalisable, namely, if they could be postulated as standing for the benefit of the entire universe. Hence, Cloots defends the promotion of French interests by arguing that there is no article in the Declaration of Rights which does not apply to all men of all climes (see Todorov 1993, p. 189). In Maurras we find a similar sophistry: 'It is a doctrinal truth, in a philosophy very remote from daily life, that the fatherland is in our day the most complete and the most coherent manifestation of humanity . . .' (cited in Todorov, 1993, p. 190). Ironically, this reasoning is unapologetically exhumed in Julia Kristeva's strange book, *Nations Without Nationalism* (1993). While Kristeva begins soundly enough with a lament about particularism, her argument gradually builds up to the conclusion that the French nation transcends the pitfalls of patriotism on account of its unique universality. In words strikingly reminiscent of Maurras she asks: 'where else one might find a theory and a policy more concerned with respect for the *other*, more watchful of citizens' rights . . . more concerned with individual strangeness?' (pp. 46–7).

Reasoned liberal thinkers have long argued that in its positive aspect nationalism—much like the family—ought to provide an education in good international manners, teaching citizens to gain their cosmopolitan bearings in the wider world. Kristeva and the thinkers examined by Todorov proceed somewhat differently, by postulating the European nation as an elastic universal project capable of accommodating the rest of the world—of raising it to the level of the mother/fatherland (see Todorov 1993, p. 254). Colonialism, thus, becomes the logical outcome or practical application of the universal ethnocentrism which characterises much late eighteenth and nineteenth century European nationalism. In a peculiar sense, it exemplifies the cosmopolitan impulse which so agitates the guilty conscience of 'enlightened' nationalisms. As Todorov writes:

> From this viewpoint, the history of humanity is confused with that of colonization—that is, with migrations and exchanges; the contemporary struggle for new markets, for supplies of raw materials is only the end result—rendered harmless owing to its origins in nature—of that first step that led the human being to cross her own threshold. The most perfected race

117

will unfailingly win, for perfection is recognised by its own ability to win battles (1993, p. 257).

Anti-colonial nationalism responds to this painful symbiosis between imperialist and nationalist thought in a variety of ways. It attempts, for instance, to be selective in its borrowings from colonialist nationalism, and it consoles itself with the understanding that while the colonial nation-State can only confer subjecthood on the colonised, the projected postcolonial nation-State holds out the promise of full and participatory citizenship. And yet, insofar as nationhood is the only matrix for political change, does the anti-colonial will-to-difference simply become another surrender to the crippling economy of the Same—'a copy of that by which it felt itself to be oppressed'? In Bernard Cohn's judgment, Indian nationalism spoke almost exclusively through the idiom of its rulers (Cohn 1983). Terence Ranger similarly maintains that African nationalisms simply dressed their radicalism in European hand-me-downs. And Edward Said reads Conrad's *Nostromo* to insist that postcolonial nation-States, more often than not, become rabid versions of their enemies: 'Conrad allows the reader to see that imperialism is a system. Life in one subordinate realm of experience is imprinted by the fictions and follies of the dominant realm' (Said 1993, p. xxi).

To what extent can we—as postcolonial critics—concede the mimetic nature of anti-colonial nationalisms, or submit to the paradox that the very imagining of anti-colonial freedom is couched in language of colonial conquest? For Chatterjee, the fault lines of Indian nationalism emerged at the very moment of its conception, in its desire to counter the colonial claim that the non-Western world was fundamentally incapable of self-rule in the challenging conditions of the modern world (Chatterjee 1993a, p. 30). Insofar as Indian nationalism prepared to embark on a project of indigenous self-modernisation, it announced its suicidal compromise with the colonial order: 'It thus produced a discourse in which, even as it challenged the colonial claim to political domination, it also accepted the very intellectual premises of "modernity" on which colonial domination was based' (Chatterjee 1993a, p. 30). As a consequence, nationalist discourse surrendered its 'meaning' to a European etymology. Accordingly, nationalist production 'merely consists of particular utterances whose meanings are fixed by the lexical and grammatical system provided by . . . the theoretical framework of post-Enlightenment rational thought' (1993a, p. 39).

Without denying the acuity of this analysis, we might proceed by foregrounding a crucial distinction between—to borrow Jayprakash Narayan's phraseology—the 'outward' attributes of nationalism and the 'mental world of those who comprise it' (Narayan 1971, p. xv). To properly pursue this separation between the people-who-comprise-the-nation and the State-which-represents-the-nation, it is useful to think of nationalism, through a literary analogy, as a genre. It is commonly understood that the nation-State is the proper end of nationalism, that is, the point at which the narrative of nation-making achieves its generic closure and therefore its distinctive generic identity. In these terms, we might say that the foundation of the postcolonial nation-State embodies the paradigmatic moment of generic conformity between anti-colonial nationalism and its antagonistic European predecessor. As Lloyd tells us, the project of State formation is 'the locus of "Western" universalism even in decolonising states', for it heralds the violent absorption of the heterogeneous nationalist imagination within the singular trajectory of world historical development (Lloyd 1993b, p. 9). Moreover, the generic continuity between anti-colonial movements and colonial regimes is sharply elucidated in the simple transference of State machinery—which marks the inaugural moment of postcoloniality. In this transfer, nationalist revolutionaries simply come to inhabit the bureaucratic machinery created for the implementation of colonial rule. And as Jayprakash Narayan has written of Congress rule in post-independence India: 'One of the more malignant features of that machine is its continued adherence to the British imperialist theory that it is the duty of the people to obey first and then to protest' (Narayan 1971, p. xviii).

As we have seen, liberal accounts of nationalism insist that the process of nationalisation is entirely congruent with the ends of the nation-State. Thus, the awakening of national consciousness is said to instantiate a teleology of inexorable rationality and development which finds its completed form in the regulative economy of the State. Nationalism, Gellner maintains, 'emerges only in the milieux in which the existence of the state is very much taken for granted' (Gellner 1983, p. 5). And yet it is obvious that the enterprise of anti-colonial nationalism invokes energies which—in Lloyd's formulation—are intrinsically *against* the apparatus of the State (see Lloyd 1993a). For anti-colonial nationalism first acquires its meaning and its impetus through the etymology of struggle, and, as writers such as Dharampal and Guha argue, this struggle is often spoken in a distinctly popular, indigenous and pre-colonial idiom (see Dharampal 1971; Guha 1983b). Thus, rather than being simply 'derivative', the insurgent moment of anti-colonial nationalism not only contradicts the pre-eminence of the State, but it also furnishes its dissent through the autonomous political imagination of the people-who-comprise- the-nation. So also there is a sense in which the recalcitrant elements, characters, and actions invoked and energised by anti-colonial nationalism are ultimately in excess of the generic closure proposed by the postcolonial nation-State (see Lloyd 1993a). And these indomitable features remain in circulation as vestigial traces of different imaginings struggling to find expression within the monotonous sameness which infects the postcolonial State. Tragically, as Dharampal points out, so long as the postcolonial State retains a certifiably colonial belief in an infallible State structure: 'It not only keeps intact the distrustful, hostile and alien stances of the state-system *vis a vis* the people but also makes the latter feel that it is violence alone which enables them to be heard' (Dharampal 1971, p. lx).

Some versions of anti-colonial thought have attempted to break this nexus between dissenting nationalism and the State. For example, Fanon remains circumspect about the desirability and creativity of the postcolonial state. His writings are almost prophetic in their predictions about the imaginative lethargy of bourgeoisie-led national governments, 'who imprison national consciousness in sterile formalism' (Fanon 1990, p. 165). In Fanon's understanding, such governments inevitably privilege the imitative scramble for 'international prestige' over and above the dignity of all citizens. Fanon's vision of a government 'for the outcasts and by the outcasts' (1990, p. 165) was reflected to a large extent in Gandhi's utopian dream of a decentralised polity. Notoriously, Gandhi desired that the Indian National Congress disband upon independence to give way to autonomous, self-sufficient and self-regulating village/local communities. Once again, nowhere did Gandhi conceive of the nation-State as the logical fruition of the anti-colonial movement. From a different perspective his friend and critic, the poet Rabindranath Tagore, retained a life-long opposition to the conformity-producing rhetoric of nationalism. For Tagore, nationalism was a system of illusions, designed progressively to homogenise and normalise small, individual sentiments of insurgency. Recently, the Nigerian Nobel laureate, Wole Soyinka, has added his voice to this committed band of dissenters. Once again, his focus is upon the 'leadership dementia' which has lead to the disintegration of the Nigerian nation (Soyinka 1996, p. 153). For Soyinka, the postcolonial nation needs to be re-imagined along the lines of its original conception, as a revolutionary and dissident space from which—indeed, through which—it was possible to refuse the totalitarianism and violence of colonial governments. This, then, is its inheritance, its responsibility to the world: 'our function is primarily to project those voices that, despite massive repression, continue to place their governments on notice' (Soyinka 1996, p. 134).

7

One world: the vision of postnationalism

In the preceding chapter an attempt was made to postulate the colonial encounter as an adversarial confrontation between two competing nationalisms. It was argued that colonialism owes at least some of its inheritance to the violent and expansionist energies of European nationalism. So also it was observed that the history of decolonisation has generally, and perhaps most effectively, been articulated through the resistant counter-energies of anti-colonial nationalism. We saw that anti-colonial revolutionaries such as Fanon and Gandhi and postcolonial critics such as Said and Parry alike concede the positive role of anti-colonial nationalisms in mobilising and organising the aspirations of oppressed and colonised peoples the world over. Nevertheless, each of these writers also tends to believe that oppositional nationalism is—or at least ought to be—a transitional and transitory moment in the decolonising project. This chapter will focus more closely on some of the theoretical and political conditions which contribute to such reservations about the permanence and versatility of anti-colonial nationalism. We will consider arguments detailing the limited political and discursive range of ethnic/racial identity and cultural nationalism, and in so doing, sketch out some features of the postcolonial engagement with the globalisation of cultures. This discussion will draw attention to the postcolonial desire for extra- or post-national solidarities, and consider concepts and terms such as 'hybridity' and 'diaspora' which have come to characterise mixed or globalised cultures.

Globalisation, hybridity, diaspora

For all its revolutionary and therapeutic benefits, there are, as Fanon has written, many pitfalls to national consciousness. Foremost among these are uncritical assertions and constructions of cultural essentialism and distinctiveness. Fanon, as Bhabha points out, 'is far too aware of the dangers of the fixity and fetishism of identities within the calcification of colonial culture to recommend that "roots" be struck in the celebratory romance of the past or by homogenising the history of the present' (Bhabha 1994, p. 9). For Fanon, as we have seen in earlier chapters, the entrenched discourse of cultural essentialism merely reiterates and gives legitimacy to the insidious racialisation of thought which attends the violent logic of colonial rationality. Accordingly, 'the unconditional affirmation of African culture' reinstates the prejudices embodied in 'the unconditional affirmation of European culture' (Fanon 1990, p. 171).

Clearly, the nationalist work of psychological and cultural rehabilitation is a crucial and historically expedient phase in the liberation of a people consigned, as Fanon puts it, to barbarism, degradation and bestiality by the harsh rhetoric of the colonial civilising mission. Nonetheless, aggressive asservations of cultural identity frequently come in the way of wider international solidarities. In Fanon's understanding, the claims of these larger and more expansive solidarities are finally more compelling than those of national culture. Ideally, national consciousness ought to pave the way for the emergence of an ethically and politically enlightened global community. The consciousness of self, Fanon writes, 'is not the closing of a door to communication. Philosophic thought teaches us, on the contrary, that it is its guarantee. National consciousness, which is not nationalism, is the only thing that will give us an international dimension' (1990, p. 199).

On a similar note, Stuart Hall, among others, is salutary in his warning that the assertions of dissident 'culturalisms' should, at best, be regarded as a necessary fiction or, as a form of 'strategic essentialism'—relevant only to the particular exigencies of the colonial encounter (see Hall 1989). After colonialism, it is imperative to imagine a new transformation of social consciousness which exceeds the reified identities and rigid boundaries invoked by national consciousness. Postcolonialism, in other words, ought to facilitate the emergence of what we might, after Said, call an enlightened 'postnationalism'. Nativism, as Said writes, 'is *not* the only alternative. There is the possibility of a more generous and pluralistic vision of the world' (Said 1993, p. 277).

The vast majority of postcolonial critics and theorists seem to agree that the discourse surrounding 'postnationalism' offers a more satisfactory reading of the colonial experience and, simultaneously, the most visionary blueprint for a postcolonial future. It is often argued that the perspective offered by anti-colonial nationalism restricts the colonial encounter to a tired impasse or opposition between repression, on the one hand, and retaliation, on the other. Notwithstanding the historical and political truth of this reciprocal antagonism, the anti-colonial perspective neglects to acknowledge the corresponding failures and fissures which trouble the confident edifice of both colonial repression and anti-colonial retaliation. Rarely did the onslaught of colonialism entirely obliterate colonised societies. So, also, far from being exclusively oppositional, the encounter with colonial power occurred along a variety of ambivalent registers.

Postnationalism pursues such indeterminacies in the colonial encounter in order to bridge the old divide between Westerner and native through a considerably less embattled—if more politically amorphous—account of colonialism as a cooperative venture (see Said 1993, p. 269). In this, it is concerned with the fulfilment of two principal objectives. First, it seeks to show how the colonial encounter contributed to the mutual transformation of coloniser and colonised. In other words, the old story of clash and confrontation is retold with an eye to the transactive/transcultural aspect of colonialism. As Harish Trivedi writes: 'it may be useful to look at the whole phenomenon as a *transaction* . . . as an interactive, dialogic, two-way process rather than a simple active–passive one; as a process involving complex negotiation and exchange' (Trivedi 1993, p. 15). Second, this gentler perusal of the colonial past produces a utopian manifesto for a postcolonial ethic, devoted to the task of imagining an inter-civilisational alliance against institutionalised suffering and oppression (see Nandy 1986). Fanon's *Wretched of the Earth* concludes with a strikingly similar, indeed prescient, vision for postcolonial futurity: 'The human condition, plans for mankind and collaboration between men in those tasks which increase the sum total of humanity are new problems, which demand true inventions' (Fanon 1990, p. 252).

Fanon's hyperbolic utopianism has found a favourable constituency among postcolonial writers of divergent theoretical persuasions. Generally speaking, there seem to be three conditions which have prepared contemporary postcolonial thought for this discursive turn toward postnationalism. First, a growing body of academic work on globalisation insists that in the face of the economic and electronic homogenisation of the globe, national boundaries are redundant or—at least—no longer sustainable in the contemporary world. The random flow of global capital is accompanied, as Arjun Appadurai writes, by an unprecedented movement of peoples, technologies and informations across previously impermeable borders—from one location to another (see Appadurai 1990). This McDonald'sisation of the world demands postcolonial attention, for in some sense, colonialism was the historical harbinger of the fluid global circuits which now—so compellingly—characterise the discomfiting propinquities of modernity. In her astute reading of imperial travel narratives, Mary Louise Pratt draws attention to the fact that colonial

Eurocentrism was engendered by a peculiarly 'planetary consciousness', which produced a 'picture of the planet appropriated and redeployed from a unified European perspective' (Pratt 1992, p. 36). The imperial gaze, in other words, delivered a distinctively globalised perception of the disparate world. In addition, albeit perversely, the colonial encounter itself accelerated the contact between previously discrete and autonomous cultures. Imperialism, as Said argues, enforced a necessary contiguity or overlap between diverse and mutually antagonistic national histories. After colonialism, the independence of India marked a crucial event in the histories of both modern India and modern Britain. The experience of empire, Said writes, 'is a common one'. Accordingly, the condition of the postcolonial aftermath pertains 'to Indians and Britishers, Algerians and French, Westerners and Africans' (Said 1993, p. xxiv). Postcoloniality, we might say, is just another name for the globalisation of cultures and histories.

A second imperative for the postnationalisation of postcolonial theory grows out of a growing critical suspicion of what we might call 'identitarian' politics. A variety of critics—whom we have encountered in earlier chapters—have detected a metropolitan hand in the preservation and perpetuation of essentialised racial/ethnic identities. Working out of Thatcherite Britain, Stuart Hall observes the insidious—and ostensibly multiculturalist—procedures whereby the convenient Othering and exoticisation of ethnicity merely confirms and stabilises the hegemonic notion of 'Englishness'. In these circumstances, ethnicity is always-already named as marginal or peripheral to the mainstream. By contrast, Englishness, or Americanness, is, of course, never represented as ethnicity (see Hall 1989, p. 227).

The metropolitan constitution of ethnicity as a 'lack' leads critics such as Rey Chow and Gayatri Spivak to question and complicate the longing 'once again for the pure Other of the West' (Spivak 1990, p. 8). Rey Chow discerns a neo-Orientalist anxiety in the anthropological desire to retrieve and preserve the pure, authentic native. In our survey of Said's work we have already encountered a reading of the parasitic relationship between Western knowledge production and the non-Western world. In the face of contemporary globalisation, Chow argues, this relationship is now under threat. The native is no longer available as the pure, unadulterated object of Orientalist inquiry—she is contaminated by the West, dangerously un-Otherable. So it is that the contemporary Orientalist blames living third-world natives for their modernity, their inexcusable 'loss of the ancient non-Western civilisation, his loved object' (Chow 1993, p. 12).

Chow's reading of the neo-Orientalist discourse of 'endangered authenticities' is wonderfully corroborated in Hanif Khureshi's recent novel *The Buddha of Suburbia*. Khureshi's Anglo-Indian hero Karim, in pursuit of thespian aspirations, agrees to participate in an audition organised by the seedy and decidedly B-grade theatre director Shadwell. As it happens, Karim's unregenerate South London accent seriously belies Shadwell's expectations of exoticism. Karim, he finds, is a culturally impoverished and disappointingly British lad who has absolutely no stories to tell about eccentric aunties and Oriental wildlife. But Karim does land a part—as Mowgli, the native protagonist of Kipling's imperialist classic. Not content to let his new actor explore the subtle nuances of his assigned role, Shadwell instructs Karim to work harder on his Indian accent, and also to smear himself with brown polish before he appears on stage. Ironically, Gayatri Spivak finds the postcolonial intellectual in a similar position to Khureshi's Karim. Where the West once insisted on the illegitimacy of non-Western knowledges, now—Spivak laments—'we postcolonial intellectuals are told that we are *too* Western' (Spivak 1990, p. 8).

And yet, as Spivak is well aware, the metropolitan investment in the pure non-West is all too often assisted by an opportunistic postcolonial scramble for the ethnic margin. 'I could easily construct', she tells us, 'a sort of "pure East" as a "pure universal" or as a "pure institution" so that I could then define myself as the Easterner, as the marginal or as specific, or as the para-institutional' (1990, p. 8). But where Spivak is able to resist the dubious appeal of marginality, lesser

127

thinkers secure their professional privileges through the discourse of 'minor-ness' and alterity. In a curious reversal of Disraeli's colonialist truism, the East—as Rey Chow points out—has become a career for the displaced Easterner. Chow writes scathingly about the language of victimisation and 'self-subalternisation' which, she argues, 'has become the assured means to authority and power' in the metropolis (Chow 1993, p. 13). This professionalisation of the margin is doubly insidious as it makes a mockery of those who must continue to fight neglected and real battles 'at home': 'What these intellectuals are doing is robbing the terms of oppression of their critical and oppositional import, and thus depriving the oppressed of even the vocabulary of protest and rightful demand' (Chow 1993, p. 13).

Thus, the critical mood of disaffection with 'identitarian' politics which we have been discussing, grows out of the conviction that the rhetoric of racial/ethnic essences has been co-opted and thereby emptied of meaning by an unwholesome partnership between neo-Orientalism and postcolonial opportunism. Correspondingly, this critique is accompanied by an urgent appeal for a new, regenerative, postcolonial politics which refuses its share in the advantages of alterity, which is willing to act in and for the world without seeking cover under the bounded signs of race/nation/ethnicity, and which, as Trinh T. Minh-ha writes, insists upon its own radical indeterminacy: 'Not quite the Same, not quite the Other, she stands in that undetermined threshold place where she constantly drifts in and out' (Trinh 1991, p. 74).

Finally, to conclude this account of the growing contiguity between postcolonialism and postnationalism, we need to consider the pervasive postcolonial exhaustion with the mantric iteration of the embattled past. This mood, à la Tina Turner, of not wanting to fight no more, is fuelled by the conviction that the adversarial basis of old solidarities lacks contemporary credence. In conservative Britain, for instance, old racial oppositions come in the way of other more urgent alliances organised along the axes of class, gender, sexuality. So also, as Hall writes, black politics can no longer be conducted in terms of an uncompromising antithesis between a bad, old, essential white subject and a new, essentially good black subject (see Hall 1989).

Said perceives a similar impasse in old national animosities. His observations spring from a particular disenchantment with the postcolonial 'rhetoric of blame' which, as he argues, is responsible for the violence and misunderstandings which come in the wake of escalated hostilities between the Western and non-Western world. The world, as he writes, 'is too small and interdependent to let these passively happen' (Said 1993, p. 20). As well, the politics of blame and ceaseless confrontation are all too often co-opted and manipulated by what we might call the postcolonial right. A host of fundamentalist and reactionary movements have, for too long, taken cover under the garb of anti-Western sentiment to, in Said's words, 'cover up contemporary faults, corruptions, tyrannies' (1993, p. 17). Finally, for all the blindness of unequivocal anti-nationalism, postcolonial theory has been susceptible to the general disillusionment with national cultures. Caught between the harsh extremes of ethnic cleansing, on the one hand, and the militaristic American purification of the un-American world on the other, postcolonialism ponders a ceasefire. Its hope, via postnationalism, is this: that it be possible to inaugurate a non-violent revision of colonial history, and that politics may become genuinely more collaborative in times to come.

Mutual transformations

As I have been arguing, postcolonialism pursues a postnational reading of the colonial encounter by focussing on the global amalgam of cultures and identities consolidated by imperialism. To this end, it deploys a variety of conceptual terms and categories of analysis which examine the mutual contagion and subtle intimacies between coloniser and colonised. In this regard, the terms 'hybridity' and 'diaspora', in particular, stand out for their analytic versatility and theoretical resilience.

By and large, the language of hybridity seems to derive its

petus from Fanon's astute reading of colonial
a catalyst for the accelerated mutation of col-
ties. It is Fanon's contention in *A Dying*
hat the unpredictable exigencies of the decolonising proj—— idically unsettle centuries-old cultural patterns in
colonised societies. The shifting strategies of anti-colonial
struggle, combined with the task of imagining a new and
liberated postcolonial future, generate a crisis within the social
fabric. As old habits give way to the unpredictable improvisations of revolutionary fervour, the colonised world submits to
the momentum of political renovation and cultural transformation. 'It is the necessities of combat', Fanon observes, 'that
give rise in Algerian society to new attitudes, to new modes
of action, to new ways' (Fanon 1965, p. 64). Accordingly, his
analysis of the Algerian Revolution underscores the accompanying revolution in the status of Algerian women and the
concomitant modification of traditional family life and values.
This period also witnesses a significant revision of customary
attitudes to science, technology and other such purveyors of
colonial modernity. While anti-colonial nationalism invokes the
myths of pure origin and cultural stability, in point of fact, as
Fanon writes, 'the challenging of the very principle of foreign
domination brings about essential mutations in the consciousness of the colonised, in the manner in which he perceives the
coloniser, in his human status in the world' (1965, p. 69).

Fanon's insistence upon the fundamental instability and
consequent inventiveness of anti-colonial conditions is
reworked by a variety of postcolonial theorists to produce the
discourse of hybridity. Most writers focus on the fact that the
political subject of decolonisation is herself a new entity,
engendered by the encounter between two conflicting systems
of belief. Anti-colonial identities, as Stuart Hall argues, do not
owe their origins to a pure and stable essence. Rather, they
are produced in response to the contingencies of a traumatic
and disruptive breach in history and culture (see Hall 1990b).
So also Homi Bhabha, albeit in more opaque prose, discerns
the emergence of a radically protean political entity at the
moment of anti-colonial insurgency. The grim polarities of the

colonial encounter, he maintains, are necessarily bridged by a 'third-space' of communication, negotiation and, by implication, translation. It is in this indeterminate zone, or 'place of hybridity', where anti-colonial politics first begins to articulate its agenda and where, in his words, 'the construction of a political object that is new, *neither the one nor the other,* properly alienates our political expectations, and changes, as it must, the very forms of our recognition of the moment of politics' (Bhabha 1994, p. 25). Mary Louise Pratt productively extends Hall's and Bhabha's analyses to argue that the coloniser—as much as the colonised—is implicated in the transcultural dynamics of the colonial encounter. For Pratt, this encounter can also be read less violently as a 'contact'—which requires a novel form of cross-communication between speakers of different ideological/cultural languages. This need for interaction within radically asymmetrical conditions of power invariably produces an estrangement of familiar meanings and a mutual 'creolisation' of identities (Pratt 1992, pp. 4–6)

The notion of 'in-between-ness' conjured up by the term 'hybridity' is further elaborated through the accompanying concept of 'diaspora'. It should be emphasised that the notion of 'diaspora' tends to lose some of its historical and material edge within postcolonial theory. Although 'diaspora' evokes the specific traumas of human displacement—whether of the Jews or of Africans scattered in the service of slavery and indenture—postcolonialism is generally concerned with the *idea* of cultural dislocation contained within this term. While 'diaspora' is sometimes used interchangeably with 'migration', it is generally invoked as a theoretical device for the interrogation of ethnic identity and cultural nationalism. Its value, much like that of its companion term 'hybridity', inheres, as Paul Gilroy points out, in the elucidation of those processes of 'cultural mutation and restless (dis)continuity that exceed racial discourse and avoid capture by its agents' (Gilroy 1993, p. 2). Accordingly, diasporic thought betrays its poststructuralist origins by contesting all claims to the stability of meaning and identity. In its postcolonial incarnation, such thought

131

reviews the colonial encounter for its disruption of native/domestic space. Thus, in Bhabha's characteristic inter- jections, colonialism is read as the perverse instigator of a new politics of 'un-homeliness'. If colonialism violently interpellates the sanctuary and solace of 'homely' spaces, it also calls forth forms of resistance which can, as Fanon observes, no longer be accommodated within the familiar crevices and corners of former abodes. In this sense, colonialism is said to engender 'the unhomeliness—that is the condition of extra-territorial and cross-cultural initiation' (Bhabha 1994, p. 9). Not surpris- ingly, diasporic thought finds its apotheosis in the ambivalent, transitory, culturally contaminated and borderline *figure* of the exile, caught in a historical limbo between home and the world. Said, more than any other postcolonial writer, submits all too easily to an over-valorisation of the unhoused, exilic intellectual: 'the political figure between domains, between forms, between homes, between languages' (Said 1993, p. 403). But as he himself recognises, all exiles do not become troublingly extra-institutional postcolonial theorists. For all those millions of violently dispossessed refugees produced in this century, there is still some reason to mourn the loss of home and of belonging. Accordingly, the notion of diaspora is least problematic when it illustrates the necessary mobility of thought and consciousness produced by the cultural adhe- sions of colonialism. As Rey Chow suggests, postcolonialism needs to focus upon the epistemological implications of 'dias- pora' and 'migrancy' in order to produce forms of knowledge which are dislocated, deterritorialised and in circulation as a 'form of interference' (Chow 1993, p. 142).

As we have seen, the happy conjunction of diasporic thought and the discourse of hybridity assists postcolonialism in its search for evidence regarding the mutual transformation of coloniser and colonised. In recent years, much postcolonial attention has focussed on questions regarding the reconfigura- tion and unsettling of Western/colonial identity. A significant incentive for work in this direction was provided by James Clifford's seminal essay 'Travelling cultures' (1992), which gestured toward the possibility of rethinking colonialism not only as the expression of settled European nationalism, but rather more interestingly as a historically nuanced culture of travel. Although the colonial adventure was predicated on a triumphant moment of 'return', it could also be read as a type of migration or diaspora which relied upon a massive movement of European populations. Indeed, as Pratt's work so persuasively argues, the experience—and accompanying narrative—of travel was instrumental in the fashioning of imperial identity. On the basis of this understanding, it then becomes possible to reverse the twin discourses of hybridity and diaspora in order to disclose the instability and adulteration of colonial culture and subjectivity.

Antony Pagden's fascinating review of Enlightenment thought draws attention to the historical anxieties of cultural impurity which accompanied the nomadic progress of colonialism (Pagden 1994). Thus, in Diderot, Pagden finds a severe denunciation of the restlessness and rootlessness which draw the colonial traveller further away from the self-defining *esprit national* of the stable metropolis. Diderot's fears for the loss of the coloniser's identity are echoed in Herder who laments the horrors of hybridity and cultural miscegenation which must attend the unnatural mingling of disparate nations. These anxieties are, in turn, framed by the familiar apprehension that colonial settlers might submit to the civilisational depravity of their victims or, in other words, 'go native'. Notably, the colonial archive itself records the administrative imperative to—at least—'appear native' in the performance of governmental power. The evangelical activities of colonial missionaries frequently required the paradoxical and threatening indigenisation of the gospel, and in colonial India, the Curzon administration chose, somewhat curiously, to proclaim its hegemony through the transculturated form of the displaced Mughal Darbar (see Cohn 1993).

Fears about the disquieting 'nativisation' of the colonial edifice also feed into speculations about the possible corruption of metropolitan culture itself by the wandering coloniser. For how, European anti-colonialists argued, could the metropolitan homeland remain immune to the products of its tyrannies abroad? As Pagden writes, 'the same routes that had carried the colonist out would also allow his vices . . . to seep back into the motherland' (Pagden 1994, p. 139). These nervous queries about the 'immorality' of colonialism uncover a central paradox at the heart of imperialism: namely, the profound discrepancy between the inflated claims of the civilising mission and the harsh reality of colonial violence. As I have argued in a previous chapter, the ethical and epistemological centre of Western rationality was effectively emptied of its meanings by the harsh progress of the colonial mission. In Gyan Prakash's words: 'the mission to spread civic virtue with military power, or propagate the text of the "Rights of Man" in the context of slave and indentured labour, could not but introduce rifts and tensions in the structure of Western power' (Prakash 1995, p. 4).

The troubling reciprocity between the metropolitan centre and the colonial periphery is sounded through the knowledge that the metropolis is not safe from the cultural contagion of its own 'peripheral' practices. This colonial world, as Said argues, circulates in the shadowy margins of most cultural narratives produced by imperialism. An attentive postcolonial rereading of these cultural texts reveals, for instance, that the civilised realm of Austen's *Mansfield Park* is sustained by the distant slave plantation of Antigua, and that Pip's economic stability in Dickens' *Great Expectations* is garnered from the remote expanses of colonial Australia. On a more literal note, the dynamic of colonial travel also brings the periphery into the centre by enforcing, in the first instance, the involuntary migration/diaspora of enslaved or indentured labour. The scattering of Africa into the West, as Alioune Diop once observed, was conducted according to the dictates of Western hegemony. Subsequent waves of voluntary and unwanted migrations continue to challenge the cultural and demographic stability of the Western world. The colonial voyage out, Said writes, has met its unsettling counterpart in the postcolonial journey in.

In this context, critics such as Bhabha and Pratt also argue that the figure of the colonised 'native' is instrumental in the contamination/hybridisation of colonial meanings. Pratt maintains that metropolitan modes of understanding are seriously confounded when the native combines a selective appropriation of colonial idioms with indigenous themes (see Pratt 1994). For Bhabha, the colonised subject is rather more ontologically incalculable. As he argues, this figure's ambivalent response to the colonial invader: 'half acquiescent, half oppositional, always untrustworthy—produces an unresolvable problem of cultural difference for the very address of colonial cultural authority' (Bhabha 1994, p. 330). Needless to say, the 'native' is herself not entirely immune to the slipperiness of her own interactions with colonialism. If the single figure of the colonised native becomes the unstable site of cross-cultural meanings and interactions, another—more significant—instability informs the *ad hoc* fabrication of wider anti-colonial solidarities. Let us not forget that the tenuous vertical solidarities of anti-colonial nationalism presuppose a unity of differences. The heterogeneous community soldered together under the shallow rubric of the postcolonial nation-State bespeaks its own political hybridity. The internal differences of the anti-colonial community, as I argued in the previous chapter, are always in excess of the postulated postcolonial nation. Stuart Hall's various observations on race politics underscore a similar heterogeneity and hybridity at the heart of 'essential' black identity. So also Paul Gilroy's magisterial work on the African diaspora highlights the irrepressible cultural diversity which goes into the making of 'black experience' and which has always informed the governing tropes of a recognisably transnational 'black aesthetics' (Gilroy 1993). There is no denying that the experience of colonial/racial oppression meets its immediate and necessary antithesis in the language of racial identity and cultural nationalism. But, as Gilroy insists, the themes of postcoloniality eventually transcend the boundaries of ethnicity and nationalism to proclaim a considerably more generous 'double consciousness' (1993, p. 1).

Postnational utopias: toward an ethics of hybridity

For all its hyperbolic claims, the discourse of hybridity and diaspora is not without its limitations. Despite postcolonial attempts to foreground the mutual transculturation of coloniser and colonised, celebrations of hybridity generally refer to the destabilising of colonised culture. The West remains the privileged meeting ground for all ostensibly cross-cultural conversations. Moreover, within the metropolis, multicultural celebrations of 'cultural diversity' conveniently disguise rather more serious economic and political disparities. In this context, it is also crucial to remain wary of claims which favour 'hybridity' as the only 'enlightened' response to racial/colonial oppression. The dangers of 'enlightened hybridity' are amply demonstrated in Ashcroft et al.'s recently announced objections to the aggressively postcolonial claims of the indigenous peoples of 'settled colonies' which, arguably, compete with the corresponding claims of 'white settler' Australians and Canadians. These critics maintain that while settler culture is able to concede its own cultural unauthenticity, indigenous groups, by contrast:

> have so often fallen into the political trap of essentialism set for them by imperial discourse . . . The result is the positioning of the indigenous people as the ultimately marginalised, a concept which reinscribes the binarism of centre/margin, and prevents their engagement with the subtle processes of imperialism (Ashcroft et al. 1995, p. 214).

By postulating the discourse of essentialism as just another unhealthy symptom of 'false consciousness', Ashcroft et al. deliver a death blow to the value of any decisively oppositional politics. But if the language of hybridity is to retain any seriously political meaning, it must first concede that for some oppressed peoples, in some circumstances, the fight is simply not over. Hybridity is not the only enlightened response to oppression.

While keeping these qualifications in mind, there is no denying that the postnational promise of a genuine cosmopolitanism remains seriously appealing. However, we need to recognise that the appeal of this discourse inheres in its unembarrassed—and potentially embarrassing—utopianism, namely, in its efforts to imagine a benevolent system of ethics in the language of hybridity. So far we have focussed our attention on the possibilities arising from a postnational rereading of the colonial encounter. In this final section, we might gesture toward some of the features which constitute this postnational ethics of hybridity.

For all its animosity, the colonial encounter produced a rich body of thought which concerned itself with a visionary commitment to the end of all institutional suffering. Much of this thought began with a critique of 'Western civilisation', but its aim—in so doing—was to instigate a reform within the very structures of Western rationality. Thus, Gandhi's uncompromising repudiation of modernity, as we saw in a previous chapter, emphasised the transcultural benefits of a non-violent sociality. The oppressors, he maintained, had to be liberated from their worst selves. And, of course, no one was better qualified for this task than the oppressed. Fanon calls upon a similar ethical commitment from the people whom he designates 'the wretched of the earth'. In his words: 'The Third World today faces Europe like a colossal mass whose aim should be to try to resolve the problems to which Europe has not been able to find the answers' (Fanon 1990, p. 253).

In a sensitive reading of this colonial archive, Ashis Nandy suggests that the future of what we have been calling a 'postnational ethic' must begin by 'recognising the oppressed or marginalised selves of the First and the Second world as civilisational allies in the battle against institutionalised suffering' (Nandy 1986, p. 348). In other words, Nandy suggests that the boundaries between colonial victors and colonised victims be replaced by a recognition of the continuity and interface between these old antagonists. Inevitably, such a move poses a challenge to the discrete and 'pure' identities of both victor and victim. Following in the footsteps of Aimé Césaire—the father of *'négritude'*—the inchoate form of postnational ethics urges the recognition that oppressors are

137

themselves the victims of their own modes of oppression. In Césaire's words: 'colonisation works to *decivilise* the coloniser, to *brutalise* him in the true sense of the word, to degrade him, to awaken him to buried instincts, to covetousness, violence, race hatred, and moral relativism' (Césaire 1972, p. 13). A muted reading of Césaire's prose draws attention to the simple fact that, and as Nandy points out, imperfect societies all too often exploit their own human instruments of oppression. In Fanon's diagnostic writing, for example, a great deal of attention is devoted to the psychological and emotional disorders of men required to perform tortures by the French colonial administration in Algeria.

This emphasis on the victimisation of the victor is not intended to elide the palpable suffering of those directly oppressed by colonialism. Rather, its objective is to facilitate a complex system of cross-identification—of ethical hybridity—connecting former political antagonists. Relatedly, an analysis of the 'contaminated' victor needs to be complemented by an analysis of the victim as a sometimes-collaborator, sometimes-competitor, with the oppressive system. As Nandy writes:

> The temptation is to use a psychological mechanism more congruent with the basic rules of the oppressive system so as to have a better scope to express one's aggressive drives. The temptation is to equal one's tormentors in violence and to regain one's self-esteem as a competitor within the same system (Nandy 1986, p. 354).

These arguments form the basis of Fanon's objection to the racialisation of thought continued by the rhetoric of anti-colonial cultural essentialism, and, as we saw in the previous chapter, the basis of wide-ranging arguments against the imitative deadlock of anti-colonial nationalisms. By foregrounding the parallel 'contamination' of the victims of colonialism, Nandy draws attention to the hybrid and unstable identities of both coloniser and colonised. Accordingly, he argues that the ethic of a postnational/postcolonial utopia can only begin to address the requirements of its inter-civilisational alliance by first conceding the contiguity between masters and slaves. In his words:

> . . . a violent and oppressive society produces its own special brands of victimhood and privilege and ensures a certain continuity between the victor and the defeated, the instrument and the target . . . As a result, none of these categories remain pure. So even when such a culture collapses, the psychology of victimhood and privilege continues and produces a second culture which is only manifestly not violent or oppressive (1986, p. 356).

In an appendix to the discussion so far, we might briefly query the larger relevance of the postnational/postcolonial ethic: does it pertain only to the exigencies of the colonial encounter and its aftermath, or does it have anything to say to ethics itself about the constitution of the ethical individual? Throughout this book, it has been my contention that postcolonial theory arises out of, and extends, the field of Western philosophy/theory. Accordingly, I believe that its accidental speculations on ethics, no less, reinforce some significant recent attempts to critique the well-worn Kantian understanding of moral agency and value. As is well known, the Kantian belief in the pre-eminence of moral value is predicated upon certain expectations of the ethical subject (Kant 1981, 1964, 1961). To be moral agents in the Kantian sense, we must rigorously stand aloof from the contingencies of our human-ness—from the domain of 'luck' which informs all the special circumstances of human nature. So, also, we must consistently maintain a strict independence from our desires and attachments at any given moment. Such a transcendental and unified ethical agent is constitutively free from the heterogeneity of her own consciousness, from the distractions of her experience. As Michael Sandel has written in his critique of Kant and Rawls:

> A self standing at a distance from the interests it has puts the self beyond the reach of experience, to make it invulnerable, to fix its identity once and for all. No commitment could grip me so deeply that I could not understand myself without it.

No transformation of life purposes could be so unsettling as to disrupt the contours of my identity. No project could be so unsettling that turning away from it would call into question the person I am (Sandel 1982, p. 62).

However, as Sandel contends, this bounded and 'pure' ethical agent ultimately inhabits a disenchanted world. For our sense of value—our moral character—is predicated upon the 'contaminating' attachments of human existence. We are fashioned by the contingencies and contradictions of our lives, and rarely does an ethical action or decision proceed from the dictates of a single imagination or a single set of feelings (see Nussbaum 1986, p. 40). The cognitively human ethical agent, as Sandel suggests, is a constitutively hybrid entity. In certain moral conditions the appropriate conception of the self would have to include its 'intersubjective' obligations: its sense of itself as embracing 'more than a single human being' (Sandel 1982, p. 62). So also we must concede the 'intrasubjective' complexity of any given self:

> . . . that for certain purposes, the appropriate description of the moral subject may refer to a plurality of selves within a single, individual human being, as when we account for inner deliberation in terms of the pull of competing identities, or moments of introspection in terms of occluded self-knowledge . . .' (1982, p. 63).

In these critiques of Kant we can begin to discern elements of what we have been calling a postnational/postcolonial ethics of hybridity. In such a guise, postcolonialism arguably has something to say to ethical thought in general. Its proposal for a non-violent reading of the colonial past through an emphasis on the mutual transformation of coloniser and colonised, and its blueprint for a utopian inter-civilisational alliance against institutionalised suffering is, indeed, salutary. The postcolonial turn to the rhetoric of postnationalism seriously humanises the world we have inherited. But, as always, we need to ensure that the euphoric utopianism of this discourse does not degenerate into a premature political amnesia.

8

Postcolonial literatures

The contesting themes of nationalism and postnationalism which we have been discussing govern the critical concerns of postcolonial literary theory. It is to this specialised branch of postcolonialism that we will now direct our attention.

Despite its interdisciplinary concerns, the field of postcolonial studies is marked by a preponderant focus upon 'postcolonial literature'—a contentious category which refers, somewhat arbitrarily, to 'literatures in English', namely, to those literatures which have accompanied the projection and decline of British imperialism. This academic privileging of postcolonial literature is informed by recent critical attempts to postulate the colonial encounter primarily as a textual contest, or a bibliographic battle, between oppressive and subversive books.

Following the impact in the mid-1980s of 'cultural materialism' upon literary theory, critical practice has been urged to concede the material underpinnings of all culture. Texts, as is now commonly agreed, are implicated in their economic and political contexts. Few critics would dispute the understanding that all literature is symptomatic of, and responsive to, historical conditions of repression and recuperation. While postcolonial literary theory invokes these cultural materialist assumptions in its account of textual production under colonial and postcolonial conditions, it goes a step further in its claim that textuality is endemic to the colonial encounter. Texts, more than any other social and political product, it is argued, are the most significant instigators and purveyors of colonial power and its double, postcolonial resistance. Thus, as Chris Tiffin and Alan Lawson insist: 'Imperial relations may have been established initially by guns, guile and disease, but they were maintained in their interpellative phase largely by textuality' (Lawson & Tiffin 1994, p. 3). Conversely, it follows that the textual offensiveness of colonial authority was met and challenged, on its own terms, by a radical and dissenting anti-colonial counter-textuality:

> Just as fire can be fought by fire, textual control can be fought by textuality . . . The post-colonial is especially and pressingly concerned with the power that resides in discourse and textuality; its resistance, then, quite appropriately takes place in—and from—the domain of textuality, in (among other things) motivated acts of reading (Lawson & Tiffin 1994, p. 10).

By recasting postcoloniality as a literary phenomenon, critics like Tiffin and Lawson implicitly, if accidentally, privilege the role and function of the postcolonial literary critic—whose academic expertise suddenly provides the key to all oppositional and anti-colonial meanings. This chapter will examine some significant literary-critical accounts of the colonial encounter. The next section will go on to counter the textual co-option of imperial history by pointing to the political limits of 'postcolonial literature'.

Textual politics

Most textual mappings of the colonial encounter take their cue from Said's monumental reading of imperial textuality. Readers may recall that Said's *Orientalism* treats European colonialism as a 'discourse', namely, as the project of representing, imagining, translating, containing and managing the intransigent and incomprehensible 'Orient' through textual codes and conventions. It is Said's contention that colonial or Orientalist discourse manifested itself as an influential system of ideas, or as an inter-textual network of interests and meanings implicated in the social, political and institutional contexts of colonial hegemony. In writing the 'Orient' through certain governing metaphors and tropes, Orientalists simultaneously underwrote the 'positional superiority' of Western consciousness and, in so doing, rendered the 'Orient' a playground for Western 'desires, repressions, investments, projections' (Said 1991 [1978], p. 8). Colonial textuality, in Said's terms, produced the 'Orient' as colonisable. Its imaginative command over the 'Orient' can, thus, be read as a rehearsal for militaristic and administrative domination. On a similar note, Elleke Boehmer's recent and lucid study of colonial and postcolonial literature describes British colonialism as a 'textual takeover' of the non-Western world (Boehmer 1995, p. 19). Her account foregrounds imperial textual production as an attempt, through writing, to domesticate the alarming alterity of 'recalcitrant peoples, unbreachable jungles, vast wastelands, huge and shapeless crowds' (Boehmer 1995, p. 94). By recasting the new colonised terrain within familiar narrative and generic moulds, colonial writing exemplified, in Boehmer's words, 'an attempt at both extensive comprehension and comprehensive control' (1995, p. 97).

Boehmer, among others, follows Said in her attention to the textual reactiveness of British colonialism. Indeed, the colonised world does appear to have driven colonisers and their wives into a frenzied verbosity which expressed itself variously in travelogues, letters, histories, novels, poems, epics, legal documents, records, memoirs, biographies, translations and censuses. And, concomitantly, the Empire itself came to define the textual self-representation and narrative sensibility of metropolitan British culture. As Said writes in *Culture and Imperialism*, imperial notations and allusions furnish the 'structures of attitude and reference' which sustain the stable world of the Victorian novel. Thus, imaginative texts achieve a double function: on the one hand they help to garner imperial possessions, and on the other, they supply national/colonial culture with an exalted self-image of its geographical and material provenance. In other words, if Orientalist texts authorise European Atlantic power over the Orient, the Victorian novel—according to Said—authorises imperialism as the bedrock of British cultural identity. Its narrative mode and fictional content prove indispensable to the consolidation of imperial authority. In Said's words: 'imperialism and the novel fortified each other to such a degree that it is impossible . . . to read one without in some way dealing with the other' (Said 1993, p. 84).

Recent studies of imperial textuality are also mindful of an alleged complicity between nineteenth-century colonial ideology and the emergence of English literature as an academic discipline in the colonies. These accounts argue that the 'English text' effectively replaced the Bible—and thereby, the evangelical ambitions of Christian missionaries—to become the most influential medium for the colonial civilising mission. As evidence for this argument, critics frequently cite Macaulay's infamous minute of 1835, which defended the introduction of 'English Education' in colonial India on the grounds that 'a single shelf of a good European Library was worth the whole native literature of India and Arabia'. Macaulay's valorisation of English literature at the cost of indigenous literatures is taken as a paradigmatic instance of canon formation. Arguably, his hierarchy of literary value establishes English literature as the normative embodiment of beauty, truth and morality, or, in other words, as a textual standard that enforces the marginality and inferiority of colonised cultures and their books. Thus, literature, as the authors of *The Empire Writes Back* insist, 'was made as central to the cultural enterprise of Empire as the monarchy was to its political formation' (Ashcroft et al. 1989, p. 3).

Gauri Viswanathan's influential book *Masks of Conquest* (1989) affirms the mutually reinforcing relationship between literary studies and British rule in India from yet another perspective. She claims that the British administration in India used English literature strategically to contain the anticipated threat of native insubordination. Fearful of a native reaction to the coercive features of direct military rule, English administrators endeavoured to 'mask' or disguise their material investments by presenting English studies as proof of their disinterested humanist commitment to the pedagogic enlightenment of their subjects. The planned dissemination of English literature, Viswanathan tells us, was intended to manage negative perceptions of empire, not only by representing colonial rule as an educational mission, but also—and more insidiously—by circulating and popularising the human face of English culture and Englishmen. In sharp contrast to the unpalatable violence of European colonialism, 'the English literary text, functioning as a surrogate Englishman in his highest and most perfect state, becomes a mask for economic exploitation . . . successfully camouflaging the material activities of the coloniser' (Viswanathan 1989, p. 20). By presenting English literature both as an opiate of the masses and also as a proxy for colonial government, Viswanathan foregrounds the controlling mechanisms of imperial textuality. In the course of her analysis, English Studies becomes—somewhat incredibly—the most substantial weapon in the colonial arsenal. As she writes: 'A discipline that was originally introduced in India primarily to convey the mechanics of language was thus transformed into an instrument for ensuring industriousness, efficiency, trustworthiness, and compliance in native subjects' (1989, p. 93).

Critics who are in agreement with Viswanathan's hypothesis likewise maintain that English Studies was instrumental in confirming the 'hegemony' or 'rule by consent' of European colonialism. Accordingly, the successful inauguration of this discipline in the colonised world is said to mark the juncture at which native populations came to internalise the ideological procedures of the colonial civilising mission. Writers like Ashcroft et al. develop this thesis in a more extravagant and metaphorical vein, by foregrounding the textual invasion, or 'interpellation', of colonised subjectivities. Thus, the eagerly assimilated English text is shown to spread the subtle infection of colonialist imperatives within the unsuspecting native body. Urged to memorise choice passages from English literary masters, the colonial child submits to the secret logic of spiritual and political indoctrination. The very 'recitation of literary texts', these critics argue, 'becomes a ritual act of obedience' (Ashcroft et al. 1995, p. 426).

These revisionist readings of colonial pedagogy are symptomatic of a prevailing mood of introspection among many 'postcolonial' English Departments. The rhetoric of suspicion surrounding English literature is matched by a range of 'syllabus reform' programs, geared toward an overhaul of the traditional Eurocentric curriculum with a view to excluding canonical offenders in favour of submerged textual 'outsiders'. A related focus on postcolonial pedagogical practice addresses questions arising from the apparent discrepancy between the antagonistic worlds of the colonial text and the postcolonial classroom. These efforts often take the form of consciousness-raising exercises directed against the ongoing 'naturalisation' of the colonial canon. Rather than permit students to pursue a mystified 'love of Shakespeare', postcolonial pedagogy undertakes to historicise the received curriculum—and inherited literary affections—with a view to revealing what Viswanathan describes as 'imperialism's shaping hand in the formation of English Studies' (Viswanathan 1989, p. 167).

Many of these recent pedagogic rumblings were anticipated by the Kenyan writer and academic Ngugi wa Thiong'o as early as 1968. In late October of that year Ngugi and some of his other colleagues in the English Department at the University of Nairobi composed a contentious paper entitled 'On the Abolition of the English Department' (Ngugi 1972). Far from settling for a mere reformation of teaching practices, Ngugi and his co-authors challenged the dubious cultural and pedagogical pre-eminence of English literature within a decolonised African context. They maintained that insofar as literature was duty-bound to illuminate the spirit animating a people, it was far more appropriate that the unauthentic discourse of Englishness be replaced by a radical centralisation

of authentically African literature and language. English literature would find a place within this new disciplinary schema,
but in keeping with its brief enrolment in African history, it
would be accommodated where it belonged—at the margins
of African culture. In colonial India, Gandhi's regular invec-
tives against English education revealed a similar belief in the
legitimate cultural primacy of Indian literatures and languages.
In anticipation of post-independence India, where English
would remain the privileged language of administration and
the ruling elite, he objected with some fervour to 'the harm
done by this education received through a foreign tongue . . .
It has created a gulf between the educated classes and the
masses. We don't know them and they don't know us' (*Collected Works* vol. 14, p. 16).

Notably, Gandhi's and Ngugi's uncompromising textual/cul-
tural inversions do not find much favour in postcolonial
literary-critical discourse. The authors of *The Empire Writes
Back*, for instance, reserve judgment about anti-colonial 'abrogation' or the unequivocal rejection, in their words, 'of the
metropolitan power over the means of communication'
(Ashcroft et al. 1989, p. 38). In the name of Fanon's famous
objections to the derivative logic of *négritude*, Ashcroft et al.
continually reiterate the well-worn postcolonial maxim that
the reversed scramble for cultural primacy only serves to
reinforce the old binaries which secured the performance of
colonial ideology in the first place. Accordingly, the categorical
refusal of imperial culture is, at best, a necessary evil in the
decolonising process. In itself, 'abrogation' or inversion represents an incomplete or failed radicalism which needs to acquire
the more subtle political habits of 'appropriation' or 'subver-
sion-from-within'. The anti-colonial 'appropriator' challenges
the cultural and linguistic stability of the centre by twisting
old authoritarian words into new oppositional meanings. Such
is the power of this creative intervention that, 'without the
process of appropriation the moment of abrogation may not
extend beyond a reversal of the assumptions of privilege, the
"normal", and correct inscription, all of which can simply be

taken over and maintained by the new usage' (Ashcroft et al. 1989, p. 38).

It is helpful to think of this stipulated shift from abrogation to appropriation as a shift from 'unlearning English', to the project of 'learning how to curse in the master's tongue'. This latter mode, in turn, marks the emergence of what we might call a 'Caliban paradigm'. Toward the beginning of Shakespeare's *The Tempest* (a play much appropriated for postcolonial ends), there is a well-known altercation between Miranda, daughter of the proto-colonial settler Prospero, and Caliban, the dispossessed (ab)original inhabitant of the island in which the play's action is located. Miranda itemises Caliban's ingratitude for her pedagogic gifts of language and, consequently, self-knowledge: 'When thou didst not, savage, / Know thine own meaning, but wouldst gabble like / A thing most brutish, I endowed thy purposes/ With words that made them known' (I.ii.355–8). In response, Caliban names but one dubious benefit of his linguistic indoctrination: 'You taught me language, and my profit on't / Is, I know how to curse' (I.ii.363–4). While the fictional Caliban speaks somewhat parodically, his speech symbolically illustrates the logic of protesting 'out of', rather than 'against', the cultural vocabulary of colonialism.

The dynamics of the 'Caliban paradigm' are seen to generate a host of creative anxieties among anti-colonial literary practitioners. Nationalist writer-appropriators must both recognise and subvert the authority of imperial textuality. They must submit to what Boehmer has perceptively called a 'double process of *cleaving*'. This schizophrenic performance involves, in her words:

> *cleaving from*, moving away from colonial definitions, transgressing the boundaries of colonialist discourse; and in order to effect this, *cleaving to*: borrowing, taking over, or appropriating the ideological, linguistic, and textual forms of the colonial power (Boehmer 1995, pp. 106–7).

Troubled by the paradox of borrowing or owning a vocabulary whose moral meanings must be repudiated or disowned, the anti-colonial writer re-enacts the overarching dilemma of nationalist thought in the colonial world. Anti-colonial nationalism, as we have seen in an earlier chapter, is also shaped by a complicated relationship of debt and defiance to Enlightenment thought. Its historical burden, as Partha Chatterjee writes, inheres in the obligation to simultaneously be 'a different discourse, yet one that is dominated by another'. And yet, as Chatterjee probes: 'How far can it succeed in maintaining its difference from a discourse that seeks to dominate it?' (Chatterjee 1993a, p. 42).

These postcolonial queries about the imaginative anxieties which accompany the emergence of anti-colonial political/literary formations bear some resemblance to Harold Bloom's earlier speculations on poetic influence. In *The Anxiety of Influence* (1973), Bloom famously absorbed Freud's account of the Oedipal struggle into literary theory, to argue that all literary activity was, in effect, the scene of a struggle between a 'beginning poet', or *ephebe*, and the crippling influence of powerful literary 'forefathers'. The *ephebe* circumvents this influence, not through an 'abrogation', but rather through a deliberate and creative misreading or misprision of literary predecessors. Thus, the moment of poetic 'departure' or 'difference' is ushered in under the guise of incomprehension—through an apparent inability to read as required.

Several assumptions in Bloom's hypothesis find their way into Homi Bhabha's feted account of 'colonial mimicry'. Taken as a general description of those colonial meanings/identities which are 'almost the same, *but not quite*' (Bhabha 1994, p. 86), mimicry designates, first, the ethical gap between the normative vision of post-Enlightenment civility and its distorted colonial (mis)imitation. Thus, in Bhabha's words: 'Between the Western sign and its colonial signification there emerges a map of misreading that embarrasses the righteousness of recordation and its certainty of good government' (1994, p. 95). But 'mimicry' is also the sly weapon of anti-colonial civility, an ambivalent mixture of deference and disobedience. The native subject often appears to observe the

149

political and semantic imperatives of colonial discourse. But at the same time, she systematically misrepresents the foundational assumptions of this discourse by articulating it, as Bhabha puts it, 'syntagmatically with a range of differential knowledges and positionalities that both estrange its "identity" and produce new forms of knowledge, new modes of differentiation, new sites of power' (1994, p. 120). In effect, then, 'mimicry' inheres in the necessary and multiple acts of translation which oversee the passage from colonial vocabulary to its anti-colonial usage. In other words, 'mimicry' inaugurates the process of anti-colonial self-differentiation through the logic of inappropriate appropriation.

In this sense, 'mimicry' has become the new slogan of postcolonial literary analysis. The emerging consensus on postcolonial literary practice has it that the most radical anti-colonial writers are 'mimic men', whose generic misappropriations constantly transgress the received and orthodox boundaries of 'literariness'. Accordingly, the paradigmatic moment of anti-colonial counter-textuality is seen to begin with the first indecorous mixing of Western genres with local content. By this reasoning, anti-colonial texts become political when, for instance, the formal shape of the European novel is moulded to indigenous realities, or when the measured sound of English is accented through an unrecognisable babel of native voices.

Most postcolonial literary critics refer to Raja Rao's *Kanthapura* (1971 [1938]) as the classic example of radical mimicry. Rao's eloquent story about the revolutionary impact of Gandhian thought upon the residents of a small Indian village begins with some famous prefatory remarks about the challenge of narrating rural India through an English idiom. The 'telling', as Rao confesses, is not 'easy': 'One has to convey in a language that is not one's own the spirit that is one's own. One has to convey the various shades and omissions of a certain thought movement that looks maltreated in an alien language' (pp. i–ii). What follows in the text is an 'adulteration' of 'proper' English with the cadences and 'tempo' of Indian speech. It is worth mentioning that Ngugi resolved a similar discrepancy between the English language and African realities through a decisive political commitment to only write in his native Gikuyu. In contrast—and conveniently for postcolonial literary theory—Rao refuses, for personal rather than political reasons, to relinquish the English language as the medium for his Indian stories. Instead, he appropriates English on the grounds that it is 'not really an alien language to us', and in so doing, he exemplifies the 'hybridity' and 'syncretism' favoured by postcolonial literary criticism. In his words, 'We cannot write like the English. We should not. We cannot write only as Indians'.

Postcolonial literary critics are agreed that writers like Rao—and unlike Ngugi—are exemplary for their refusal merely to replace a Western cultural paradigm with its non-Western counterpart. If Rao's 'mimic' mode subverts the authority of imperial textuality, it also forecloses, once and for all, any appeal to an 'authentic' or 'essential' Indian-ness. Thus positioned as the iconic emblem of an indeterminate hybridity, the anti-colonial nationalist writer is now eagerly absorbed into a critique of third-world cultural nationalism.

Accounts of postcolonial counter-textuality begin by affirming the contiguity between the anti-colonial novel and anti-colonial nationalism. In general, postcolonial theory subscribes whole-heartedly to Benedict Anderson's insistence upon the textual underpinnings of nation-ness. It is Anderson's contention that nations are imaginative and cultural artefacts rather than empirical and scientific entities. They are imagined into coherence because 'the members of even the smallest nations never know most of their fellow-members, meet them, or even hear of them, yet in the minds of each lives the image of their communion' (Anderson 1991 [1983], p. 6). The novel and the newspaper are, in this context, the two principal print forms capable of containing and representing, in one place, the impossible diversity that is the nation. Thus, the novel becomes a sort of proxy for the nation. Its pages communicate, in Anderson's words, 'the solidity of a single community, embracing characters, author and readers, moving onward through calendrical time' (1991 [1983], p. 27). In keeping with

Anderson's assertions, critics like Fredric Jameson argue that the emergent third-world novel is especially committed to the rendition of nationalist realities (Jameson 1986). It is certainly the case that the newly discovered textures of realist prose in colonies like India, quickly lent themselves to the sociopolitical concerns of nationalism. In addition, socialist anti-colonial thought sanctioned the view that cultural/literary 'labour' was indispensable to the nationalist task of social transformation. In other words, the anti-colonial novelist was often, although not always, a nationalist.

And yet postcolonial literary theory rarely applauds nationalism as a feature of the counter-textuality of the anti-colonial writer/novelist. Far from conceding that the anti-colonial novel authenticates the anti-colonial nation, it argues that this novel irrevocably dilutes the imaginary essence of the nation through a Western dialect. If nation-ness is itself engendered within a colonial grammar, its narration in the novel form is, thus, doubly derivative. Seen in these terms, the quintessential 'hybridity' of the anti-colonial novelist/writer demonstrates that, as Ashcroft et al. maintain, 'it is not possible to return to or to rediscover an absolute pre-colonial cultural purity, nor is it possible to create national or regional formations entirely independent of their historical implication in the European colonial enterprise' (Ashcroft et al. 1989, pp. 195–6). Much like the nation she narrates, this novelist becomes the Janus-faced bearer of a split consciousness or a double vision. Apart from the 'impurity' of her cultural influences, the anti-colonial writer also suffers from the cultural alienation endemic to the nationalist elite in general. Anti-colonial nationalists, as Boehmer writes, 'often tended to have more in common with the middle-class counterparts in other colonies struggling for self-representation than with the disenfranchised masses of their own countries' (Boehmer 1995, p. 114). In the hands of such story-tellers, cultural nationalism does not really stand a chance. Accordingly, the syncretic narrative, celebrated by postcolonial critics, becomes a distorting mirror in which the anti-colonial nation is forced to recognise its own estrangement.

The textual mapping of the colonial encounter, which we

have been discussing, concludes with the new 'migrant' novel. It is often argued that the counter-textual mood of anti-colonial or nationalist writing finds its apotheosis in the cosmopolitan restlessness of writers such as Salman Rushdie, Ben Okri, Michael Ondaatje and Bharati Mukherjee. Postcolonial literary theory, as we have seen, tends to privilege 'appropriation' over 'abrogation' and multicultural 'syncretism' over cultural 'essentialism'. While the anti-colonial novel is shown to betray these symptoms despite itself, the 'migrant' novel is entirely explicit in its commitment to hybridity. Positioned on the margins or interstices of two antagonistic national cultures, it claims to open up an in-between space of cultural ambivalence. As Homi Bhabha writes in his gloss on Derek Walcott, such writing refuses (is unable?) to 'oppose the pedagogy of the imperialist noun to the inflectional appropriation of the native voice', preferring instead, 'to go beyond such binaries of power in order to reorganise our sense of the process of identification in the negotiations of cultural politics' (Bhabha 1994, p. 233). Edward Said is also eloquent in his praise of the nomadic energies of such writers, whom he sees as transgressing the confinement of both imperial and provincial orthodoxies. The migrant novel is inaccessible, then, to the possessive prose of cultural nationalism. So also its transculturated narrative is postulated as a serious challenge to the cultural stability of the metropolitan centre. In Said's words: 'The authoritative, compelling image of empire . . . finds its opposite in the renewable, almost sporty discontinuities of intellectual and secular impurities, mixed genres, unexpected combinations of tradition and novelty' (Said 1993, p. 406). Whereas the anti-colonial novel tentatively appropriated the language of empire from afar, writers like Rushdie are believed to transform—from within—the geographical and imaginative space of the Western metropolis. In conclusion, Rushdie's tropicalised London—parodically renamed *Ellowen Deeowen*—may well be, as Bhabha writes, an unrecognisable terrain, distorted 'in the migrant's mimicry' (Bhabha 1994, p. 169). But whether this mimicry can be taken as the highpoint of postcolonial politics is a question that we might address, more critically, in the next section.

Postcolonial texts, anti-colonial politics

The textual mapping of the colonial encounter relies upon a narrative of competing or contesting textualities. In these terms, all colonial texts are seen as repressive, and on the other side of the binary, all postcolonial/migrant texts are invested with radically subversive energies. Moreover, following the controversy surrounding the publication of *The Satanic Verses*, Salman Rushdie has emerged as the paradigmatic exponent of migrant (textual) dissidence, as the voice, in other words, of postcolonial heterodoxy. Notwithstanding the individual insights of postcolonial literary theorists, this account of the colonial encounter suffers from some serious conceptual inadequacies and political evasions.

In the first place, we need to qualify the generalising assumption that all colonial texts are repressive. The colonial, as Boehmer writes, 'need not always signify texts rigidly associated with the colonial power' (Boehmer 1995, p. 4). In a previous chapter we already discussed the limits in Said's account of Orientalist texts. Far from always-already collaborating with the material investments of colonialism, several Orientalists laboured to counter the ethnocentric assumptions of metropolitan culture. Relatedly, the Orientalism of sexual dissidents like Carpenter and Forster was predicated upon an idealistic understanding of the East as a utopian alternative to the ethical and political violence of empire. On a different note, Boehmer draws attention to the fact that colonial texts very often betrayed the uncertainties and anxieties of empire. Colonialist writing, in her words, 'was never as invasively confident or as pompously dismissive of indigenous cultures as its oppositional pairing with postcolonial writing might suggest' (1995, p. 4). And, just as colonial writing was not unequivocal in its affirmation of empire, the pedagogic circulation of the 'English text' in the colonies did not necessarily secure the compliance of native subjects and the concomitant hegemony of European colonialism.

While accounts of colonial pedagogy are consistently sensitive to the intentions of colonial administrators, they remain oblivious to the complex and complicating reception of the English text in the colonial world. Gauri Viswanathan, for instance, confidently claims that 'it is entirely possible to study the ideology of British education quite independently of an account of how Indians actually received, reacted to, imbibed, manipulated, reinterpreted, or resisted the ideological content of British literary education' (Viswanathan 1989, p. 11). Even if we concede, as Viswanathan suggests, the self-sufficient enclosure of colonial systems of representation, an account of the material effects of colonial ideology and pedagogy is surely incomplete in the absence of *any* reference to the recipients of English education. In this regard, we might briefly draw attention to the selective literary 'taste' of Indian readers, to their confident judgment of the European canon and, finally, to the threatening critical facility with which native students approached their curriculum.

The anti-colonial archive suggests that rather than being the passive objects of an authoritarian and alien pedagogy, Indian readers remained obdurately selective in their response to the English syllabus. Viswanathan herself provides the untheorised example of some Calcutta citizens whose petition for a properly English education was accompanied by the disclaimer that 'they would take that which they found good and liked best' (Viswananthan 1989, p. 43). Especially noteworthy is the unauthorised receptivity of Indian readers to the Romantic poets in general, and Shelley in particular. Indeed, Shelley's canonisation in Sri Aurobindo's book *The Future Poetry* as the 'sovereign voice of the new spiritual force that was at the moment attempting to break into poetry' (Sri Aurobindo 1991, p. 125), goes entirely against the grain of contemporary English critical opinion. *The Future Poetry*, which was first serialised between 1917 and 1920, also deserves attention more generally for its comprehensive and often very critical account of British literary history.

Aurobindo's survey of European literature is animated by various reservations about the literary worth of the Elizabethan dramatists, Milton, and the 'Augustans'—whom he holds responsible for 'the death of the true poetic faculty' (1991, p. 88).

This active response to English literature is but one example of the interpretative autonomy and acumen of native readers and students. There is evidence to suggest that this accomplished reader/student was soon perceived as a threat by the colonial administration. Notably, when Sir George Campbell, Lieutenant-Governor General of Bengal in 1871 to 1874, introduced riding and walking tests for candidates applying for the subordinate civil services, there was a general consensus, and fear, that Indian applicants would effortlessly excel in the written and literary component of the exam. Physical endurance was another matter, and Sri Aurobindo was among the many 'effete' Bengali intellectuals whose bureaucratic aspirations were thwarted by an inability to pass the riding test.

If imperial textuality finds one of its limits in the critical response of anti-colonial readers, the obligatory subversiveness of postcolonial literature is seriously limited by the notion of 'textual politics' favoured by postcolonial literary theory. In a move which effectively replaces politics with textuality, such theory delivers a world where power is exclusively an operation of discourse, and resistance a literary contest of representation. Not content with what Said has called the necessary 'worldliness' of texts, the rhetoric of textual politics enters into a competitive and antagonistic relation with the realm of the 'social'. For instance, Homi Bhabha's theoretical invitation to acknowledge 'the force of writing' slips into a passionate defence of textuality 'as a productive matrix which defines the "social" and makes it available as an objective of and for action'. Textuality, he insists, 'is not simply a second-order ideological expression or a verbal symptom of a pre-given political subject' (Bhabha 1994, p. 23). Bhabha's textual bias is shaped by a quite legitimate and eloquent resistance to the crippling dichotomy between theory and activism. However, such are the overcompensations of his prose, that his cogent defence of the political relevance of thought tends to give way to an unsustainable assertion of textual pre-eminence. Thus, in the beginning—before the first murmuring of political consciousness—we find the word, and the word is with postcolonial writing. Bhabha's insistent claim that 'the political subject—as indeed the subject of politics—is a discursive event' (1994, p. 23), anticipates a theoretical model where textuality starts to elide the materiality and contingency of the world itself.

When textual politics becomes doctrinal in this way, it starts to treat the text as an end in itself, or as an improvement upon the hopeless inadequacy of political realities. Jonathan White's close reading of postcolonial fiction in an essay entitled 'Politics and the individual in the modernist historical novel' offers a telling example of this tendency. White claims that the postcolonial novel is the last repository of revolutionary consciousness in a world increasingly bereft of political and historical content. In this regard, the work of writers like Nadine Gordimer and Salman Rushdie may, he argues, have a major role to play in 'redressing such an inadequacy' (White 1993, p. 209). In making these contentions, White not only favours the novel for its pedagogic capacity to disseminate political information but also, and more disturbingly, suggests that we might start to think of 'the novel as an alternative way of *doing* history and politics' (1993, p. 209). Thus, we acquire a new perspective on Rushdie's *Midnight's Children*, whereby the novel's textual plenitude compensates for its author's view of India's political and historical impoverishment. The novel, White concedes, offers an uncompromising and 'pessimistic perspective about India' (p. 237)—an account of nationalist failure and historical 'grotesquery'. But, in his words, 'one other reality, the teeming inventiveness of consciousness and hence of narration, constantly lightens that burden, which would otherwise be intolerable' (p. 237). Notwithstanding the stunted historicity of the Indian nation, we can still gain solace from the fact that India is 'equally embodied in . . . the positive growth of the text' (p. 237). So, where Bhabha permits writing to prefigure the 'social', White

157

gives it the licence to disfigure political realities. Rushdie's narration is valorised at the cost of the world he narrates. After *Midnight's Children*, we may rest assured that 'India, is not solely (in the old cliché) a teeming begetter of peoples but, also, a begetter of teeming narrative' (p. 238).

White's textually obsessed analysis of *Midnight's Children* is partly motivated by the curious political and historical circumstances which have made Rushdie into the emblematic figure of textual politics. In the face of the Ayatollah Khomeini's *fatwa*, *The Satanic Verses* has emerged as a 'textual event'—and Rushdie's teeming narrative does indeed deliver a writing which, in White's words, 'is full of risk' (p. 228). Any liberally motivated response to Rushdie's painful predicament would defend his right to write. Nevertheless, it is possible to recognise Rushdie's decision to go on writing and publishing as unmistakably political, without claiming self and language as the last locus of political agency.

In a sense, Rushdie's own textual absorption of politics owes its inheritance to the deep political evasiveness which characterises the bourgeois English novel. Here we find that a similar investment in textual coherence and narrative style has replaced the grittiness of the political. In an instructive essay, Simon During offers some relevant comments regarding Edmund Burke's influence on the unmotivated prose of this genre. Burke, During tells us, 'locates liberty not in thought, not in national will, ultimately not even in tradition, but, almost unawares, in a personal freedom embedded in the act of writing. It goes without saying that to find liberty there is not to require socio-political change, it is barely to find liberty at all' (During 1990, p. 146). While it would be foolish to push the analogy between Burke and Rushdie, the postcolonial universalisation of Rushdie's predicament does produce a similar mishandling of 'liberty'. Rushdie's personal freedom is, indeed, chronically and inescapably embedded in writing. But the concerns of the world about which he writes exceed the exertions of textual *jouissance*. Decolonisation, as Boehmer puts it, can never be focused primarily at a discursive level . . . the struggle for selfhood is much more than the subject of self-reflexive irony. In a third-world context, self-legitimisation depended, and depends, not on discursive play but on a day to day lived resistance, a struggle for meanings which is in the world as well as on paper (Boehmer 1995, pp. 221–2).

At the outset of this chapter it was argued that postcolonial literary theory owes its preliminary politicisation of textuality to 'cultural materialism'. In its subsequent textual investments, however, it starts to betray the influence of yet another theoretical/critical genealogy, which requires some elaboration. Deconstruction is, of course, the immediate and obvious precursor for the postcolonial turn toward textuality. As is well known, Derrida's influential reclamation of writing begins with a rejection of the bias toward speech which underpins Western metaphysics. Logocentric metaphysics, Derrida tells us, has traditionally *repressed* writing itself and, concomitantly, 'suppressed for essential reasons, all free reflection on the origin and status of writing' (see Norris 1982, p. 29). Positioned thus, as the unheeded victim of Western epistemology, writing announces its revolutionary counter-claims. In Derrida's hands, the anarchic scene of textual dissemination begins to contest all embedded hierarchies of value and meaning. From now on it is texts alone which will puncture the narcissism of Western knowledge. As Norris writes in his commentary on Derrida: 'Writing is that which exceeds—and has the power to dismantle—the whole traditional edifice of Western attitudes to thought and language' (Norris 1982, p. 29). Seen through this Derridean vector, it is not surprising that postcolonial literary theory seeks its anti-colonial counter-narrative in the written word. But we might also note—and we have discussed this more fully in a previous chapter—that deconstruction itself stands charged of the political evasions which trouble its followers. A variety of critics have attributed the textual focus of deconstruction to the political disenchantment produced by the cataclysmic events of 1968. For Eagleton, the valorised deconstructive text becomes a convenient proxy for political action. In his somewhat ascerbic words: 'Unable to break the structures of state power, post-structuralism found it possible instead to subvert the structures of language. Nobody, at least, was likely to beat you over the head for doing so' (Eagleton 1983, p. 142).

From deconstruction, then, postcolonial literary theory receives an ambivalent inheritance: on the one hand, it learns to glean and defend the radical energies of writing and, on the other, it acquires the habit of investing texts with values that cannot be located or fulfilled in reality. And it is here that we can begin to discern the hidden symptoms of New Criticism—that suppressed discourse which inhabits the secret enclaves of both postcolonial and poststructuralist literary theory. For our purposes, it is enough to acknowledge that the New Critics postulated the poetic text as a sacrosanct object, hermetically sealed from the contaminations of both rational enquiry and the materialistic world which occasioned such enquiry. Seen as such, the literary text projected an alternative—a newer, better and improved world where the privileged reader could discover a refuge from, and a resistance to, the encroachments of modern industrial society. As is well acknowledged—and here, we need to stretch our genealogy even further back in time— New Criticism is itself informed by a specifically Romantic understanding of the poetic word. And it is within Romanticism, I would like to argue, that postcolonial literary theory finds its particular textual provenance. Much like New Criticism after it, the Romantics, as Eagleton puts it, discover in literature, 'one of the few enclaves in which the creative values expunged from the face of English society by industrial capitalism can be celebrated and affirmed' (Eagleton 1983, p. 19). So also, if literature compensates for the inadequacies of the world, the poetic 'imagination' and 'creative faculty' are now endowed with the political energies necessary for the work of social transformation. The poet/writer, in other words, is fashioned as a revolutionary *par excellence*.

This postulation of Romanticism as the 'originary moment', if you like, of textual politics, is particularly pertinent. For in the textual obsessions of postcolonial literary theory we might read the first symptoms of a process whereby metropolitan culture obtains a specifically 'romantic' investment in postcolonial literature and its migrant writers. These texts/writers are often seen to embody energies and values allegedly lacking or under threat in the postcolonial world. And these values, as we have seen already, are animated by a single concept, namely, 'hybridity'.

In fact, a distinctly 'romantic' vocabulary marks the prose of several postcolonial literary theorists. A collection of essays entitled: *Recasting the World: Writing After Colonialism* (ed. J. White 1995) professes its overarching concern with the 'notion of recasting realities through writing' (p. ix). Its editor, Jonathan White, locates in the postcolonial text the potential to both cope with the 'terrors' of the colonial aftermath, and engender an improved ethico-political future. Accordingly, Nadine Gordimer is cited to elaborate 'more fully the workings of transformative powers unleashed by mere words on the page (p. 2). In a similar gesture, Derek Walcott's commitment to poetic composition becomes an act of 'ongoing political commitment in its own right'—a creative antidote to counter 'every prevailing individual and societal tendency to decompose' (p. 5). White discerns, in a writer like Walcott, echoes of Blake—pre-eminent among the Romantics for his belief in the ameliorative agency of the poetic imagination. The authors of *The Empire Writes Back* find in the novels of Trinidadian writer Michael Antony a similar demonstration of 'the transformative power of the imagination' (Ashcroft et al. 1989, p. 97). So also, their analysis of the Guyanese novelist and critic, Wilson Harris, is inflected by a strikingly romantic vocabulary: 'cultures must be liberated from the destructive dialectic of history, and imagination is the key to this. Harris sees imaginative escape as the ancient and only refuge of oppressed peoples, but the imagination also offers possibilities of escape from the politics of dominance and subversion' (Ashcroft et al. 1989, p. 35).

Notably, while these accounts 'romanticise' the postcolonial writer's vision for 'marginalised' postcolonial societies, they simultaneously insist—as evident in the title of Ashcroft et al.'s volume—that postcolonial texts characteristically 'write back to' the metropolitan centre. Thus, metropolitan culture designates itself as the privileged addressee—the chosen audience—of the romantic postcolonial text. Indeed, as critics like Timothy Brennan, among others, argue, the privileged postcolonial text is typically accessible and responsive to the aesthetic and political taste of liberal metropolitan readers. The principal pleasures of this cosmopolitan text accrue from its managed exoticism. It is both 'inside' and 'outside' the West— its appropriative modality delivers new stories in reassuringly old ways. Paradoxically, and as Brennan observes, the writers whom Western reviewers select as 'the interpreters and authentic public voices of the Third World', have invariably numbered those who:

> allowed a flirtation with change that ensured continuity, a familiar strangeness, a trauma by inches. Alien to the public that read them because they were black, spoke with accents or were not citizens, they were always like that public in tastes, training, repertoire of anecdotes, current habitation (Brennan 1989, p. ix).

Read in this light, the discourse of literary hybridity becomes a sort of guilty political rationalisation of readerly preference. And it is in the attempt to make the 'cosmopolitan' or 'migrant' writer authentically representative of the 'third world' that postcolonial literary theory becomes dangerously prescriptive. Thus, the pages of a volume such as *The Empire Writes Back* assume an instructive tone with regard to the 'appropriate' form of postcolonial literature. Throughout this book, we encounter the following imperatives (with my emphasis): '*all* postcolonial literatures are cross-cultural' (Ashcroft et al. 1989, p. 39); 'the postcolonial text is *always* a complex and hybridised formation' (p. 110); 'colonialism *inevitably* leads to a hybridisation of culture' (p. 129); 'hybridity is the primary characteristic of *all* post-colonial societies whatever their source' (p. 185); 'it is *not possible* to return to or rediscover an absolute pre-colonial cultural purity' (p. 196). In its striking resistance to the possible heterogeneity of postcolonial experience and literary production, this discourse is painfully and ironically evocative of Orientalism. Moreover, its rigid directives and injunctions exhibit the stark procedures of canon formation. As with any other emergent canon, Ashcroft et al.'s selection of the best and most representative postcolonial texts is predicated upon the systematic exclusion of others. In the main, their theoretical embargo falls most heavily upon any 'located' or 'situated' literatures, namely, those which are not written in English, and those which—as we have been arguing—lay any claim to cultural alterity and authenticity. Hence, the claim that literatures in, for instance, regional Indian languages are entirely on par with the 'quantity and quality of the work in English', is met with the following response: 'This may well be the case, though until much more extensive translations into English from these languages have been produced it is difficult for non speakers of these languages to judge' (p. 122). But what does 'judgment' refer to here—what is being judged and by whom? In the face of this bias against the slightest symptoms of linguistic/cultural difference, postcolonial literary theory clears a privileged space for the voice of what Brennan has called anti-colonial liberalism.

The emergence of this voice is marked by a shift away from the old 'realist novel' of the revolutionary middle classes toward its antagonist—the new 'bourgeois novel'. Much like its historical predecessor, which During names the novel of the civil imaginary, this new narrative is characterised by a dislocation from, indeed, antagonism toward, the nation form (see During 1990). Notably, and in a characteristically deconstructive gesture, Bhabha invites such writing to 'disseminate'—and render rhetorical—the solidity and force of national culture. His theoretical faith is reserved only for those 'counter-narratives of the nation that continually evoke and erase its totalising boundaries—both actual and conceptual—disturb those ideological manoeuvres through which "imagined communities" are given essentialist identities' (Bhabha 1994, p. 149). Accordingly, far from producing the nation out of its fictional plenitude, the postcolonial novel endeavours, instead, to betray the fictionality of nationhood. In Rushdie's *Midnight's Children*, the nation is narrated by an imposter—whose

163

unreliable narration systematically distorts the chronology and significance of national history. So also *Shame* gives the lie to the national achievements of Pakistan—leaving in its place, a hollow and corrupt landscape, bereft of hope and meaning.

The evacuated and fictional space of nationalism is now animated by the new fictions of exile and migrancy. But we might pause here to consider Sara Suleri's suggestion that 'perhaps it is time for critical discourse to examine more rigorously the idiom of exile, in order to determine how inevitably its language must accrue a vertiginous absence of responsibility' (Suleri 1992, p. 184). To put this differently, need we concede the necessary 'politics of migrancy'? Especially when we consider that the migrancy of writers like Rushdie is predicated upon the luxuries of mobility. Already, Bhabha's catalogue of the new migrant sensibility enumerates only the limited resources of high-capitalist urban art that few have access to; the 'eye of the aeroplane', 'a Warhol blowup, a Kruger installation, or Mapplethorpe's naked bodies' (Bhabha 1990, pp. 6–7) do not constitute the staple culture of most migrants. So also, as Aijaz Ahmad has written:

> Among the migrants themselves, only the privileged can live a life of constant mobility and surplus pleasure, between Whitman and Warhol as it were. Most migrants tend to be poor and experience displacement not as cultural plenitude but as torment; what they seek is not displacement but, precisely, a *place* from where they might begin anew, with some sense of a stable future. Postcoloniality is also, like most things, a matter of class (Ahmad 1995, p. 16).

In the absence of any solidarities—whether nationalist or socialist—the postcolonial novel finds its provenance in the small pleasures of subjectivity; its content is almost entirely shaped by personal journeys, attachments, memories, losses. Accordingly, it seems more than a little curious that these iterative and skilful portraits of artists as young—and not so young—men should be authorised to represent the public voice of the postcolonial world. The problem is compounded when we consider that, albeit mistakenly, Rushdie's *The Satanic*

Verses stands charged of 'literary colonialism' by the very world he allegedly delivers in a radical counter-narrative to empire. Here is a pre-eminently 'hybrid' text which has exacerbated the very polarities and binaries which it is discursively obliged, if not equipped, to refuse. The controversy following the *fatwa* has only served to revive the tired dichotomies between Western civilisational plenitude and non-Western lack. Indeed, Rushdie himself invokes a similar rhetoric in his open letter to Rajiv Gandhi, written in response to India's pre-emptive proscription of *The Satanic Verses*:

> The right to freedom of expression is at the very foundation of any democratic society, and at present, all over the world, Indian democracy is becoming something of a laughing stock. When Syed Shahabuddin and his fellow self-appointed guardians of Muslim sensibility say that 'no civilised society' should permit the publication of a book like mine, they have got things backwards. The question raised by the book's banning is precisely whether India . . . can any more lay claim to the title of a civilised society (see Appignanesi & Maitland 1990, p. 35).

Rushdie's invective against India here—composed well before the imposition of the *fatwa*—is, in a sense, characteristic of his larger oeuvre. This is not to suggest that postcolonial writing is obliged to be unthinkingly 'patriotic'. Rather, we might consider the fact the Rushdie's narrative renditions of the Indian nation have always been pathologically and unequivocally reductive. What he offers in novel after novel is a lament, or a complaint against the culture he has eschewed for the transitions of migrancy. Once again, Suleri is instructive in her claim that the postcolonial imperative to invert the terms of Orientalist myth-making produces a narrative written 'in a context of romance gone wrong, a context that does not lead to the evocative absence of romance, but to the horror of Conrad's imperial parable' (Suleri 1992, p. 182). This, then, is the governing paradox of the postcolonial canon: that metropolitan culture has acquired a romantic investment in a literary narrative which is markedly *anti-romantic* in its perception of the postcolonial world. Here we can only find the language of critique; a hybridity that is predicated precisely upon an abrogation of the postcolonial nation. And yet, despite the influential liberal enmity toward nationalism, this abstract and imaginary force bears, as argued earlier, the traces of countless histories of struggles—histories which, in turn, continue to inform the ethical apparatus of countless peoples. And as During writes, 'To reject nationalism absolutely or to refuse to discriminate between nationalisms is to accede to a way of thought by which intellectuals—especially postcolonial intellectuals—cut themselves off from effective political action' (During 1990, p. 139).

Without seeking to determine the shape of an alternative orthodoxy, we might still observe that perhaps what postcolonial literature needs is a properly romantic modality; a willingness to critique, ameliorate and build upon the compositions of the colonial aftermath. It is possible, in other words, to envision a transformed and improved future for the postcolonial nation. We might conclude with the journalistic romanticism which underwrites the *Times of India*'s rejoinder to Rushdie:

> No, dear Rushdie, we do not wish to build a repressive India. On the contrary, we are doing our best to build a liberal India, where we can all breathe freely. But in order to build this India, we have to preserve the India that exists. That may not be a pretty India, but it's the only India we have (Appignanesi & Maitland 1990, p. 209).

Is this where a counter-narrative to the postcolonial counter-narrative might begin?

9

The limits of postcolonial theory

In conclusion, it could be said that postcolonialism is caught between the politics of structure and totality on the one hand, and the politics of the fragment on the other. This is one way of suggesting that postcolonial theory is situated somewhere in the interstices between Marxism and postmodernism/poststructuralism. It is, in a sense, but one of the many discursive fields upon which the mutual antagonism between these competing bodies of thought is played out. Seen as such, postcolonialism shifts the scene of this long-standing contestation to the so-called 'third world'.

The meta-narrative of colonialism

Postmodern/poststructuralist commentators argue that postcolonialism is in danger of becoming yet another totalising method and theory. On the other side, Marxist and materialist critics have vociferously made the charge that postcolonial analysis lacks the methodological structure, and will to totalise, necessary for right thinking and left politics. As we have seen, the debate about 'totalities' and 'fragments' is ultimately concerned with the status of knowledge, ethics and politics in the

167

contemporary world and, less grandiosely, within the set of disciplines which constitute the humanities.

At one extreme, and similarly to feminism, postcolonialism approaches such questions of epistemology and agency universally; that is to say, as questions which are relevant to a generalised 'human condition' or a 'global situation'. Just as feminist theory/criticism is 'one branch of interdisciplinary inquiry which takes gender as a fundamental organising category of experience' (Greene & Kahn 1985, p. 1), postcolonialism of the sort defended by the authors of *The Empire Writes Back* takes colonialism, or more specifically, European colonialism, as a way to organise the experience of 'more than three-quarters of the people living in the world today' (Ashcroft et al. 1989, p. 1). As is now well known and well acknowledged, feminism has been forced to concede that 'woman' as a monolithic category of analysis across classes and cultures fails—in Chandra Mohanty's words—to account for 'women—real, material subjects of their collective histories' (Talpade Mohanty, 1994). Experience, in other words, is crisscrossed by determinants other than those of gender or, we might add, colonialism alone.

The postcolonial deference to the homogenising and all-inclusive category 'colonialism' fails, first, to account for the similarities between cultures/societies which do not share the experience of colonialism. Second, and similarly to feminism, it fails to account for differences, in this case the culturally and historically variegated forms of both colonisation and anti-colonial struggles. As Aijaz Ahmad writes in one of his many critiques of matters postcolonial: 'the fundamental effect of constructing this globalised trans-historicity of colonialism is one of evacuating the very meaning of the word and dispersing that meaning so wide that we can no longer speak of determinate histories of determinate structures . . .' (Ahmad 1995, p. 9). This sort of semantic vacuum is most evident in the claim, made by some Australian and Canadian commentators, that settler societies stand in the same relationship to colonialism as those societies which have experienced the full force and violence of colonial domination. Such claims entirely neutralise, in the name of subject formation, the widely divergent logics of settlement and struggles for independence. Equally, they confer a seamless and undiscriminating postcoloniality on both white settler cultures and on those indigenous peoples displaced through their encounter with these cultures. For postcolonial critics like Helen Tiffin, accordingly, disparate societies such as Bangladesh and Australia are unified upon the somewhat dubious premise that their 'subjectivity has been constituted in part by the subordinating power of European colonialism' (Adam & Tiffin 1991, p. vii).

Tiffin's faith in the notion of a uniformly subordinated subjectivity invites contestation, not least of all because both subjectivity and power are so differently and unevenly inflected across cultures and histories. While 'subjectivity', in Tiffin's usage, seems to point to the state of creative 'interiority', this term also refers to the condition through which people are recognised as free and equal—or 'full'—individuals within civil society. As it happens, the story of political subjectivity has always been fraught by exclusions of gender, race, class, caste and religion. Civil society has consistently refused admission and participation to those who, in Carole Pateman's words, 'lack the attributes and capacities of "individuals"' (Pateman 1988, p. 6). Thus, for Rosseau, women were exempted from subjectivity and for Cecil Rhodes, likewise, black Africans were to be denied the benefits of 'mature' and 'full' individuality: 'The native is to be treated as a child and denied franchise. We must adopt the system of despotism . . . in our relations with the barbarous of South Africa' (cited in Nandy 1992, p. 58). Similar divisions marked the edifice of colonial government in India. As Chatterjee says: 'The only civil society that the government could recognise was theirs; colonised subjects could never be its equal members' (Chatterjee 1993b, p. 24). In this case, racial difference, much as sexual difference, becomes synonymous with political difference. Thus, unlike the colonisers who possess the privileges of citizenship and subjectivity, the colonised exist only as subjects, or as those suspended in a state of subjection. In India, the nationalist

169

struggle begins as a repudiation of this second-rate civil society of subjects—as a struggle for subjectivity.

The arguments of writers like Ashcroft, Tiffin and Griffiths fail to convince primarily on account of their refusal to address adequately the ideological wedge between histories of subjectivity and histories of subjection. There is a fundamental incommensurability between the predominantly cultural 'subordination' of settler culture in Australia, and the predominantly administrative and militaristic subordination of colonised culture in Africa and Asia. A theory of postcolonialism which suppresses differences like these is ultimately flawed as an ethical and political intervention into conditions of power and inequality. Equally, pious protestations of postcoloniality from once-colonised nations such as India must engage with the differences between internal histories of subordination, kept in place by the continuing exclusions of postcolonial civil society.

The end of colonialism

Critics such as Robert Young have recently suggested that postcolonialism can be best thought of as a critique of history (see Young 1990). This is a contentious claim and one which has been vigorously debated between Marxist and postmodernist/poststructuralist commentators. While Marxist theorists have been unequivocally dismissive of the postcolonial allergy to history, their opponents, as we have seen, have responded by including Marxism itself into their critique of historicism or historical reasoning.

The postcolonial chapter of the debate on history has a number of complex ramifications. In summary, however, a variety of postcolonial commentators have argued that 'history' is the discourse through which the West has asserted its hegemony over the rest of the world. This idea becomes clearer when we consider that Western philosophy, at least since Hegel, has used the category of 'history' more or less synonymously with 'civilisation'—only to claim both of these categories for the West, or more specifically, for Europe. In Hegel's notorious formulation, civilisation—and by implication history—moves West. The unhappy corollary to this assertion is that Western imperialist expansion has all too often been defended as the pedagogical project of bringing the 'under-developed' world into the edifying condition of history. Colonialism, in terms of this logic, is the story of making the world historical, or, we might argue, a way of 'worlding' the world as Europe. Hence the situation where, in Dipesh Chakrabarty's words, 'Europe remains the sovereign, theoretical subject of all histories, including the ones we call "Indian", "Chinese", "Kenyan", and so on' (Chakrabarty 1992, p. 1). The postcolonial/poststructuralist intervention into this problem focuses accordingly on 'history' as the grand narrative through which Eurocentrism is 'totalised' as the proper account of all humanity. Accordingly, postcolonial historiography declares its intention to fragment or interpellate this account with the voices of all those unaccounted for 'others' who have been silenced and domesticated under the sign of Europe.

Against these claims, some critics have complained that certain versions of postcolonial analysis simply reinstate the exclusionary systems of universal history. Anne McClintock develops this critique by arguing that the prefix 'post' in postcolonialism confers on colonialism 'the prestige of history proper . . . Other cultures share only a chronological and prepositional relation to a Euro-centred epoch that is over (post) or not yet begun ("pre")' (McClintock 1992, p. 3). Thus, despite its oppositional claims, postcolonial historiography runs the risk of paradoxically reunifying the diversity and alterity of the colonised world under the sign and spectre of Europe—forcing all temporalities and cultures into a hyphenated relationship with colonialism. In other words, postcolonialism semantically delivers the idea of a world historicised through the single category of colonialism. There are several negative implications which follow on from here.

Most evidently, the organisation of the immediate past under the rubric of colonialism tends to reduce the contingent and random diversity of cultural encounters and non-encounters within that past into a tired relationship of coercion and retaliation. According to Tiffin, for instance, postcolonialism consists of two 'archives' which are produced, first, 'by the subordinating power of European colonialism', and second, through 'a set of discursive practices, prominent among which is resistance to colonialism' (Adam & Tiffin 1991, p. vii). Seen as such, 'colonialism' supplies a category through which history becomes coherent, and therefore knowable, as a movement between imperial subordination and anti-colonial resistance. While there is no denying that the colonial encounter is marked by the story of Western dominance and resistances to it, we also need to acknowledge that this story is endlessly complicated by the failure, inadequacy and refusal on both sides of dominance and resistance. By attending more carefully to the silence of the archive we need to interrogate this construction of history as certain knowledge, to ask, in other words: 'Who gets known in and as history?'—or—'Who are those groups and events of whom "colonial" history is ignorant?'.

These are some of the questions asked of colonial historiography by the Subaltern Studies collective. Briefly, we might refer to their suggestion that it is primarily within elite institutions—whether colonial or nationalist—that 'history' acquires visibility and structure. Writers within this collective argue that the archival version of 'colonial' history frequently fails to accommodate or speak to the opaque and contradictory processes which characterise the politics of the people. These politics comprise, in Dipesh Chakrabarty's words, those 'plural and heterogeneous struggles whose outcomes are never predictable, even retrospectively, in accordance with schemas which seek to naturalise and domesticate this heterogeneity' (Chakrabarty 1992, p. 20). One of the reasons why such struggles remain undocumented at the institutional sites where history proper is produced is because their functional unpredictability very often causes them to swerve from the ideals of proper insurgency. As Ranajit Guha writes: 'Blinded by the glare of a perfect and immaculate consciousness the historian sees nothing, for instance, but solidarity in rebel behaviour and fails to notice its Other, namely, betrayal' (Guha 1983, p. 40). In a footnote to the argument so far, we might also add that the postcolonial binary of coercion/retaliation not only minimises the function of what Simon During speaks of as 'the consent of the colonised to colonialism' (During 1992, p. 95), but equally and perhaps more significantly, it obscures the role of those people and groups whom Ashis Nandy describes as the 'non-players' (Nandy 1983, p. xiv). By this Nandy means both the 'other' West which refuses to participate an imperial world view, and the non-West which is able to live with this alternative West, 'while resisting the loving embrace of the West's dominant self' (p. xiv.) In the spirit of the Subaltern Studies project, Nandy takes care to distinguish these non-Western non-players from the recognisable subjects of history proper, namely, 'the standard opponents of the West, the counterplayers [who] are not, in spite of their vicious rhetoric, outside the dominant model of universalism' (p. xiv). Unfortunately, the frequent postcolonial elision of 'non-players'—Western and non-Western—disablingly ignores those countless, unrecorded histories of affect, conversation and mediation; in other words, histories of what Gandhi calls *ahimsa*, or non-violence.

Moreover, to continue this critique of postcolonial 'world history', the notion of an academic 'post'-colonialism carries within it a suggestion of cognitive mastery—a detached perspective or vantage point from which it is possible to discern and to name the completed and clear shape of the past as colonialism. In this sense, the textual incoherence of history can be said to acquire meaning and definition only through the retrospective and unifying gaze of the postcolonial critic. Implicit here is the idea—central to the assumptions of optimistic philosophy and universal history—that clarity occurs progressively in time. Docherty summarises this view as being based on the conviction that:

> the meaning of an event is not immediately apparent, as if it were never present-to-itself: its final sense—to be revealed as the necessity of goodness—is always deferred . . . and thus

always different (or not what it may appear to the local eye caught up in the event itself) (Docherty 1993, p. 9).

Docherty's summary points to a theory of meaning that consists in the movement away from immediacy/particularity towards distance/universality—arguably, the ground covered by the 'post' in 'postcolonialism'. Insofar as this movement towards meaning may also be seen as one through which politics attains to theory, postcolonialism, of the sort I have been discussing so far, runs a double danger. On the one hand, it leaves itself open to the charge of depoliticisation, and on the other—and somewhat more seriously—by appearing to monopolise the privileged space of theory it can very often be seen to deny theoretical self-consciousness to the playing and non-playing participants in 'colonial time'.

Finally, whenever postcolonialism identifies itself with the epochal 'end' of colonialism, it becomes falsely utopian or prematurely celebratory. The problem, once again, arises from the term itself. As Anne McClintock argues, the term postcolonialism is haunted by an unacknowledged commitment to the principle of linear time and therefore to the idea of 'development' implicit in this view of time (McClintock 1992, p.2). The teleological promise of linear time—that is to say, its belief in the benign purposiveness of history and nature—carries within it the double charge of Progress and Perfectibility. We might argue, accordingly, that the 'post' in 'postcolonialism' invests the meaning of simple chronological succession with the utopian charge of progressiveness. The prefix 'post', in Lyotard's words, 'indicates something like a conversion' (Lyotard 1992, p. 90)—it suggests a change of heart and the emergence of a new and better world. More specifically, it produces the illusion of an enlightened supersession of colonial trouble and, in Simon During's words, it gestures toward 'a historical break which is healing gaps and struggles between North and South, developed and underdeveloped, and so on' (During 1992, p. 88). Needless to say, this suggestion of an improved and unified world order fails to account either for the increased divisiveness between and

within contemporary societies, or for the persistence of colonial formations the world over. Equally, it ignores problems of
'neocolonialism'—held in place by transnational corporations
and the international division of labour, linking first-world
capital to third-world labour markets.

A parallel concern is that the postcolonial utopia or
notional 'new world' continues to be spoken through a Western lexicon and vocabulary. We may recall, for instance,
George Bush's aggressive 'new world order' through which the
world is increasingly nuanced and assimilated as America, and
in the name of which the Gulf War was rationalised. Less
offensively, the tendency in postcolonial theory to simply, and
wishfully, extend European categories beyond colonial meanings also occurs, as During argues, 'when academic
subdisciplines, founded on a certain Eurocentrism, transmute
towards the new order—when for instance, studies in "Com-
monwealth Literature" or "New Literatures in English"
become studies in "post-colonial literature"' (During 1992, p.
96). In this guise, postcolonialism may continue—although
with the best intentions—to simply deliver old wine in new
bottles.

The influential work of Ashcroft et al. once again provides
an example of this sort of accidental elision. These commentators describe postcoloniality euphorically, as 'an
unprecedented assertion of creative activity' in those societies
which emerged after the 'dismantling' of British imperial power
(Ashcroft et al. 1995, p. 1). At the same time, they seem to
insist that this new postcolonial creative assertiveness is not so
much a gesture, however flawed, towards a cultural difference,
as it is a cultural compromise, produced through the encounter
between colonial structures and indigenous processes. In their
words, 'Post-colonial literatures are a result of this interaction
between imperial culture and the complex of indigenous practices . . . imperial language and local experience' (1995, p. 1).
The language used by these writers sets up, albeit inadvertently,
an implicit hierarchy between imperial structure/language/
culture on the one hand and indigenous process/practice/
experience on the other. So also the imperial contribution to

175

the process of cultural collaboration seems to claim all the attributes of 'theory', that is to say, those categories which shape thought and facilitate meaning. Somewhat starkly on the other side stands the raw material of indigeneity—the empirical substance of experience and practicality waiting to be shaped into theoretical self-consciousness. Ashcroft et al.'s crucial distinctions between empire and indigeneity can also be clarified in terms of the Saussurian categories of *parole*, or actual speech, and *langue*, or the objective grammar of signs which makes speech possible in the first place. By carelessly insinuating the priority of a European *langue* over and above the possibility of non-European *parole*, these critics once again repeat the tired colonialist assumption that it takes the West—in the shape of either theory or history —to bring the 'rest' to the condition of intelligibility. In this guise, postcolonialism becomes little more than the benign face of colonial rationality or, to return to Lyotard's notes on the meaning of 'post', a false rupture which 'is in fact a way of forgetting or repressing the past, that is to say, repeating it and not surpassing it' (Lyotard 1992, p. 90).

But of course, as Lyotard adds, 'post' does not have to signify movements of amnesia and repetition; it is also equipped to furnish 'a procedure in "ana-": a procedure of 'analysis, anamnesis, anagogy and anamorphosis which elaborates an 'initial forgetting' (p. 90). In its reflective modality, thus, postcolonialism also holds out the possibility of thinking our way through, and therefore, out of the historical imbalances and cultural inequalities produced by the colonial encounter. And in its best moments it has supplied the academic world with an ethical paradigm for a systematic critique of institutional suffering. So, after such knowledge, what forgiveness?

Bibliography

Adam, I. & Tiffin, H. (eds) 1991, *Past the Last Post: Theorizing Postcolonialism and Postmodernism*, Harvester Wheatsheaf, Hemel Hemstead

Ahmad, A. 1992, *In Theory: Classes, Nations, Literatures*, Oxford University Press, Oxford

——1995, 'The politics of literary postcoloniality', *Race and Class*, vol. 36, no. 3, pp. 1–20

Anderson, B. 1991, *Imagined Communities: Reflections on the Origin and Spread of Nationalism*, 2nd edn, Verso, London

Appadurai, A. 1990, 'Disjuncture and difference in the global cultural economy', *Public Culture*, vol. 2, no. 2, pp. 15–24

Appiah, K. A. 1992, *In My Father's House: Africa in the Philosophy of Culture*, Methuen, London

Appignanesi, L., Maitland, S. 1990, *The Rushdie File*, Syracuse University Press, Syracuse

Arnold, M. 1965 *The Complete Prose Works*, ed. H. H. Super, University of Michigan Press, Ann Arbor

Ashcroft, B., Griffiths, G., Tiffin, H. 1989, *The Empire Writes Back: Theory and Practice in Postcolonial Literatures*, Routledge, London

——(eds) 1995, *The Postcolonial Studies Reader*, Routledge, London

Bakshi, P. K. 1990, 'Homosexuality and Orientalism: Edward Carpenter's journey to the East', in *Edward Carpenter and Late*

Victorian Radicalism, ed. Tony Brown, Prose Studies Special Issue, vol. 13, no. 1, pp. 151–77

Barker, F., Hulme, P. & Iversen, M. (eds) 1994, *Colonial Discourse/Postcolonial Theory*, Manchester University Press, Manchester

——(eds) 1986, *Literature, Politics and Theory: Papers from the Essex Conference 1976–84*, Methuen, London

Barr, P. 1976, *The Memsahibs: The Women of Victorian India*, Secker & Warburg, London

Bauman, Z. 1991, *Modernity and Ambivalence*, Polity Press/Blackwell, Oxford

Bauman, Z. 1992, *Intimations of Postmodernity*, Routledge, London & New York.

Bernauer, J. & Mahon, M. 1994, 'The ethics of Michel Foucault', in *The Cambridge Companion to Foucault*, ed. Gary Gutting, Cambridge University Press, Cambridge

Bhabha, H. 1986, 'The other question: difference, discrimination and the discourse of colonialism', in *Literature, Politics & Theory*, eds Francis Barker, Peter Hulme, Margaret Iversen, Methuen, London, pp. 148–73

——1990, *Nation and Narration*, Routledge, London

——1994, *The Location of Culture*, Routledge, London

Bloom, H. 1973, *The Anxiety of Influence: A Theory of Poetry*, Oxford University Press, New York

——1994, *The Western Canon: The Books and Schools of the Ages*, Papermac/Harcourt Brace & Co., New York

Boehmer, E. 1995, *Colonial and Postcolonial Literature*, Oxford University Press, Oxford

Bove, P. 1985, *Intellectuals at War: Genealogies and Intellectuals*, Columbia University Press, New York

Bowie, M. 1991, *Lacan*, Harper Collins/Fontana, London

Brennan, T. 1989, *Salman Rushdie and the Third World: Myths of the Nation*, St Martins Press, New York

——1992, 'Places of mind, occupied lands: Edward Said and philology', in *Edward Said: A Critical Reader*, ed. Michael Sprinker, Blackwell, Oxford, pp. 74–95

Brewer, A. 1980, *Marxist Theories of Imperialism: A Critical Survey*, Routledge & Kegan Paul, London

Burton, A. 1994, *Burdens of History: British Feminists, Indian Women, and Imperial Culture, 1865–1915*, University of North Carolina Press, Chapel Hill & London

Butler, C. 1977, *G. W. F. Hegel*, Twayne Publishers, Boston

Campana, A. 1946 'The origin of the word "Humanist"', *Journal of the Warburg and Courtauld Institutes*, vol. 9, pp. 60–73

Cannadine, D. 1983, 'The context, performance and meaning of ritual: the British monarchy and the "invention of tradition", c. 1820–1977', in *The Invention of Tradition*, eds Eric Hobsbawm & Terence Ranger, Canto/Cambridge University Press, Cambridge, pp. 101–64

Cantimori, D. 1934, 'Rhetoric and politics in Italian humanism', *Journal of the Warburg Institute*, vol. 1, pp. 83–104

Césaire, A. 1972, *Discourse on Colonialism*, trans. Joan Pinkham, Monthly Review Press, New York

Chabran, A. 1990, 'Chicana/o studies as oppositional ethnography', *Cultural Critique*, vol. 4, no. 3, pp. 228–47

Chakrabarty, D. 1992, 'Postcoloniality and the artifice of history: who speaks for "Indian" Pasts?', *Representations*, vol. 37, pp. 1–26

——1993, 'Marx after Marxism: history, subalterneity and difference', *Meanjin*, vol. 52, no. 3, pp. 421–34

——1995, 'Radical histories and question of Enlightenment rationalism', *Economic and Political Weekly*, vol. 30, no. 14, pp. 751–9

Chambers, I. 1987, 'Maps for the metropolis: a possible guide to the present', *Cultural Studies*, vol. 1, no. 1, pp. 1–21

——1996, *The Post-Colonial Question: Common Skies, Divided Horizons*, Routledge, London

Chatterjee, P. 1992, 'Their own words? An essay for Edward Said', in *Edward Said: A Critical Reader*, ed. Michael Sprinker, Blackwell, Oxford, pp. 194–220

——1993a, *Nationalist Thought and the Colonial World: A Derivative Discourse*, 2nd edn, Zed Books, London

——1993b, *The Nation and its Fragments: Colonial and Postcolonial Histories*, Princeton University Press, Princeton, New Jersey

Chow, R. 1993, *Writing Diaspora: Tactics of Intervention in Contemporary Cultural Studies*, Indiana University Press, Bloomington

Clifford, J. 1988, *The Predicament of Culture: Twentieth-Century Ethnography, Literature and Art*, Harvard University Press, Cambridge, Massachusetts

——1992, 'Travelling cultures', in *Cultural Studies*, eds Lawrence Grossberg, Cary Nelson, Pamela Treichler, Routledge, New York, pp. 96–112

Cohn, B. 1993, 'Representing authority in Victorian England', in *The Invention of Tradition*, eds E. Hobsbawm & T. Ranger, Canto/Cambridge University Press, Cambridge, pp. 165–210

Curtius, E. R. 1953, *European Literature and the Latin Middle Ages*, trans. William D. Trask, Routledge & Kegan Paul, London

Deane, S. 1990, 'Introduction', in *Nationalism, Colonialism and Literature*, A Field Day Co. Book, University of Minnesota Press, Minneapolis, pp. 3–19

Deleuze, G. & Guattari, F. 1986, *Kafka: Toward a Minor Literature*, trans. Dana Polan, University of Minnesota Press, Minneapolis

Derrida, J. 1974, 'White mythology: metaphor in the text of philosophy', *New Literary History*, vol. 6, no. 1, pp. 7–74

Dharampal, 1971, *Civil Disobedience and Indian Tradition, With Some Early Nineteenth Century Documents*, Sarva Seva Sangh Prakashan, Varanasi

Dirlik, A. 1994, 'The postcolonial aura: third world criticism in the age of global capitalism', *Critical Inquiry*, vol. 20, pp. 328–56

Docherty, T. 1993, *Postmodernism: A Reader*, Harvester Wheatsheaf, Hemel Hempstead

During, S. 1990, 'Literature—nationalism's Other? The case for revision', in *Nation and Narration*, ed. Homi Bhabha, Routledge, London, pp. 135–153

——1992, 'Post-colonialism', in *Beyond the Disciplines: The New Humanities*, ed. K. K. Ruthven, Papers from the Australian Academy of the Humanities Symposium, no. 13, Canberra, pp. 88–100

Eagleton, T. 1983, *Literary Theory: An Introduction*, Blackwell, Oxford

Fanon, F. 1965, *A Dying Colonialism*, trans. Haakon Chevaliar, Grove Press, New York

——1967, *Black Skin, White Masks,* trans. Charles Lam Markmann, Grove Press, New York

——1990, *The Wretched of the Earth*, 3rd edn, trans. Constance Farrington, Penguin, Harmondsworth

Featherstone, M. 1988, 'In pursuit of the postmodern: an introduction', *Theory, Culture, Society*, vol. 5, nos. 2–3, pp. 195–216

Forster, E. M. 1979, *A Passage to India*, ed. Oliver Stallybrass, Penguin, Harmondsworth

Foucault, M. 1970, *The Order of Things: An Archaeology of the Human Sciences*, Routledge, London

——1972 [1989], *The Archaeology of Knowledge*, trans. A.M. Sheridan Smith, Routledge, New York

——1977, *Language, Counter-Memory, Practice: Selected Essays and Interviews by Michel Foucault*, ed. Donald F. Bouchard, Cornell University Press, Ithaca

——1977 [1987], *Discipline and Punish: The Birth of the Prison*, trans. Alan Sheridan, Penguin, Hammondsworth

——1978 [1984], *History of Sexuality*, vol. 1, trans. Robert Hurley, Penguin, Harmondsworth

——1980a, *Power/Knowledge: Selected Interviews and Other Writings 1972–1977*, ed. Colin Gordon, Harvester Press, Hertfordshire

——1980b, 'George Canguilhem: philosopher of error', *Ideology and Consciousness*, no. 7, pp. 53–4

——1984a, 'What is Enlightenment', in *The Foucault Reader: An Introduction to Foucault's Thought*, ed. Paul Rabinow, Penguin, Harmondsworth, pp. 109–122

——1984b, 'Nietzsche, genealogy, history', in *The Foucault Reader*, ed. Paul Rabinow, Penguin, Harmondsworth, pp. 76–100

——1987, 'The Order of Discourse', in *Untying the Text: A lost-structuralist reader*, ed. Robert Young, Routledge & Kegan Paul, London

——1989, 'Practicing Criticism', in *Politics, Philosophy, Culture: Interviews and Other Writings, 1977–1984* Michel Foucault, ed. Lawrence Kritzman, trans. Alan Sheridan, Routledge, New York

Fox, R. 'East of Said', in *Edward Said: A Critical Reader*, ed. Michael Sprinker, Blackwell, Oxford, pp. 144–56

Frow, J. 1990, 'The social production of knowledge and the discipline of English', *Meanjin*, vol. 29, no. 2, pp. 353–67

Gandhi, M. K. 1938, *Hind Swaraj*, reprint, Navjivan Publishing House, Ahmedabad

——1982, *The Collected Works of Mahatma Gandhi*, vols. 1–90, Ministry of Information and Broadcasting, Ahmedabad

Garin, E. 1965, *Italian Humanism: Philosophy and Civic Life in the Renaissance*, trans. Peter Manz, Blackwell, Oxford

Gay, P. 1977, *The Enlightenment, an Interpretation: The Science of Freedom*, vol. 2, W. W. Norton & Co., New York

Gellner, E. 1983, *Nations and Nationalism*, Cornell University Press, Ithaca

Gendzier, I. 1973, *Frantz Fanon: A Critical Study*, Pantheon, New York

Gilroy, P. 1993, *The Black Atlantic: Modernity and Double-Consciousness*, Verso, London

Gilson, E. (ed.) 1963, *Modern Philosophy: Descartes to Kant*, Random House, New York

Gramsci, A. 1978, *Selections from Political Writings 1921–1926*, trans. Quentin Hoare, International Publishers, New York

Greene, G. & Kahn, C. 1985, 'Feminist scholarship and the social construction of woman', in *Making a Difference: Feminist Literary Criticism*, eds Gayle Greene and Coppélia Kahn, Methuen, London, pp. 1–36

Guha, R. (ed.) 1982, *Subaltern Studies*, vol. 1, Oxford University Press, Delhi

——1983a, 'The prose of counter-insurgency', *Subaltern Studies: Writings on South Asian History and Society*, vol. 2, pp. 1–42

—— 1983b, *Elementary Aspects of Peasant Insurgency in Colonial India*, Oxford University Press, Oxford

——1992, 'Discipline and mobilise', *Subaltern Studies: Writings on South Asian History and Society*, eds Partha Chatterjee & Gyanendra Pandey, vol. 7, pp. 64–120

Gunew, S. 1990, *Feminist Knowledge: Critique and Construct*, Routledge, London

Habermas, J. 1972, *Knowledge and Human Interests*, trans. Jeremy J. Shapiro, Heinemann, London

Hall, S. 1989, 'New ethnicities' in *Black Film, British Cinema*, ICA Documents 7, Institute of Contemporary Arts, London

——1990a, 'Cultural identity and diaspora', in *Identity, Community, Culture, Difference*, ed. J. Rutherford, Lawrence & Wishart, London, pp. 222–37

——1990b, 'The emergence of cultural studies and the crisis of the humanities', *October*, vol. 53, pp. 11–23

Halliburton, D. 1981, *Poetic Thinking: An Approach to Heidegger*, University of Chicago Press, Chicago

Hegel, G. F. W. 1910, *The Phenomenology of Mind*, 3 vols, trans. J. B. Baille, Macmillan Co., London

——1975, *Lectures on the Philosophy of World History: Introduction*, trans. H. B. Nisbet, Cambridge University Press, Cambridge

Heidegger, M. 1977, 'Letter on humanism', in *Martin Heidegger: Basic Writings*, ed. David Farrel Krell, Routledge & Kegan Paul, London

Hobsbawm, E. J. 1987, *The Age of Imperialism*, Weidenfeld & Nicolson, London

——1990, *Nations and Nationalism Since 1780: Programme, Myth, Reality*, Cambridge University Press, Cambridge

Hobsbawm, E. J. & Ranger, T. 1983, *The Invention of Tradition*, Canto/Cambridge University Press, Cambridge

Holst Peterson, K. 1984, 'First things first: problems of a feminist approach to African literature', *Kunapipi*, vol. 6, no. 3, pp. 35–47

Jameson, F. 1986, 'Third-world literature in the era of multinational capitalism', *Social Text*, vol. 5, no. 3, pp. 65–88

——1990, 'Modernism and imperialism', in *Nationalism and Colonial Literature*, ed. Seamus Deane, A Field Day Co. Book, University of Minnesota Press, Minneapolis, pp. 43–68

——1991, *Postmodernism or, the Cultural Logic of Late Capitalism*, Duke University Press, Durham

Jayawardena, K. 1995, *The White Woman's Other Burden: Western Women and South Asia During British Rule*, Routledge, New York

Jones, W. 1991, 'A grammar of the Persian language', in *Sir William Jones: A Reader*, ed. Satya S. Pachori, Oxford University Press, Delhi

Kant, I. 1981, *Grounding for the Metaphysics of Morals*, trans. James Ellington, Hackett Publishing Co, Indianapolis

——1964, *The Metaphysics of Virtue; Part II of the Metaphysics of Morals*, trans. James Ellington, Hobbs-Mernl Co, Indianapolis

——1961, *Kant's Critique of Practical Reason and Other Works on the Theory of Ethics*, trans. H.J. Paton, Hutchinson University Library, London

Kaplan, C. 1985, 'Pandora's box: subjectivity, class and sexuality in socialist and feminist criticism', in *Making a Difference: Feminist Literary Criticism*, eds Gayle Greene & Coppélia Kahn, Methuen, London, pp. 146–76

Khureshi, H. 1990, *The Buddha of Suburbia*, Faber & Faber, London & Barton

Kristeva, J. 1977, *About Chinese Women*, trans. Anita Barrows, London, Marion Boyers

——1993, *Nations Without Nationalism*, trans. Leon S. Roudiez, Columbia University Press, New York

Lacan, J. 1977, *Ecrits. A Selection*, ed. Alan Sheridan, Tavistock Publications/Norton, London

Lawson, A., & Tiffin, C. (eds) 1994, *Describing Empire: Postcolonialism and Textuality*, Routledge, London

Levinas, E. 1994, 'Ethics as first philosophy', in *The Levinas Reader*, ed. Sean Hand, Blackwell, Oxford

Lloyd, D. 1985, 'Arnold, Ferguson, Schiller: aesthetic culture and the politics of Aesthetics', *Cultural Critique*, vol. 2, pp. 137–69

——1993a, 'Nationalisms against the State: towards a critique of the anti-nationalist prejudice', in *Re-examining and Reviewing the Philippine Progressive Vision*, eds Forum for Philippine Alternatives, Diliman, Quelon City

——1993b, *Anomalous States: Irish Writing and the Post-Colonial Moment*, Duke University Press, Durham

Lyotard, Jean-Francois 1991, *The Inhuman: Reflections on Time*, trans. Geoffrey Bennington & Rachel Bowlby, Stanford University Press, Stanford

——1992, *The Postmodern Explained to Children: Correspondence 1982–1985*, eds Julian Pefanis & Morgan Thomas, Power Publications, Sydney

——1993, *The Postmodern Condition: A Report on Knowledge*, trans. Geoff Bennington and Brian Massumi, University of Minnesota Press, Minneapolis

Marangoly George, R. 1993, 'Homes in the Empire, empires in the home', *Cultural Critique*, vol. 26, pp. 95–128

Marx, K. 1973, *Surveys from Exile*, ed. David Fernbach, Pelican, London

Marx, K. & Engels, F. 1975, *Collected Works of Karl Marx and Friedrich Engels*, 47 vols., Lawrence & Wishart, London

Mayo, K. 1986, *Mother India*, Indian edn, Anmol Publications, Delhi

McClintock, A. 1992, 'The angel of progress: pitfalls of the term "Postcolonialism" ', *Social Text*, Spring 1992, pp. 1–5

——1995, *Imperial Leather: Race, Gender and Sexuality in the Colonial Contest*, Routledge, London

Mehta, V. 1977, *Mahatma Gandhi and his Apostles*, Andre Deutsch, London

Memmi, A. 1968, *Dominated Man: Notes Toward a Portrait*, Orion Press, London

Nairn, T. 1977, *The Break-Up of Britain: Crisis and Neo-Nationalism*, New Left Books, London

Nandy, A. 1983, *The Intimate Enemy: Loss and Recovery of Self Under Colonialism*, Oxford University Press, Delhi

——1986, 'Oppression and human liberation: toward a post-Gandhian utopia', in *Political Thought in Modern India*, eds Thomas Pantham & Kenneth L. Deutsch, Sage, New Delhi, pp. 347–59

——1992, *Traditions, Tyranny and Utopias: Essays in the Politics of Awareness*, Oxford University Press, Delhi

——1995, *The Savage Freud and Other Essays on Possible and Retrievable Selves*, Princeton University Press, Princeton, New Jersey

Narayan, J. P. 1971 'Foreword', in *Civil Disobedience and Indian Tradition*, Dharampal, pp. xv–xx

Ngugi wa Thiong'o 1972, *Homecoming: Essays on African and Carribean Literature, Culture and Politics*, Heinemann, London

Norris, C. 1982, *Deconstruction: Theory and Practice*, Methuen, London

Nussbaum, M. C. 1986, *The Fragility of Goodness: Luck and Ethics in Greek Tragedy and Philosophy*, Cambridge University Press, Cambridge

Pagden, A. 1994, 'The effacement of difference: colonialism and the origins of nationalism in Diderot and Herder', in *After Colonialism*, ed. Gyan Prakash, Princeton, University Press, Princeton, New Jersey, pp. 124–52

Parry, B. 1987, 'Problems in current theories of colonial discourse', *Oxford Literary Review*, vol. 9, nos. 1–2, pp. 27–58

——1994, 'Resistance theory/theorising resistance, or two cheers for nativism', in *Colonial Discourse/Postcolonial Theory*, eds Francis Barker et al., Manchester University Press, Manchester, pp. 172–96

Pateman, C. 1988, *The Sexual Contract*, Polity Press, Cambridge

Pathak, Z., Sengupta, S., Purkayastha, S. 1991, 'The prisonhouse of Orientalism', *Textual Practice*, vol. 5, no. 2, pp. 195–218

Porter, D. 1983, '*Orientalism* and its problems', in *The Politics of Theory*, eds Francis Barker, Peter Hulme, Margaret Iversen, University of Essex, Colchester, pp. 179–93

Prakash, G. (ed.) 1995, *After Colonialism: Imperial Histories and Postcolonial Displacements*, Princeton University Press, Princeton, New Jersey

Pratt, M. L. 1992, *Imperial Eyes: Travel Writing and Transculturation*, Routledge, London

——1994, 'Transculturation and autoethnography: Peru 1615–1980', in *Colonial Discourse/Postcolonial Theory*, eds Francis Barker et al. Manchester University Press, Manchester, pp. 24–47

Ranger, T. 1993, 'The invention of tradition in colonial Africa', in *The Invention of Tradition*, eds E.J. Hobsbawm and T. Ranger, Canto/Cambridge University Press, Cambridge, pp. 211–62

Rao, R. 1971, *Kanthapura*, 2nd edn, Orient Paperbacks, Delhi

Rosselli, J. 1980, 'The self-image of effeteness: physical education and nationalism in nineteenth-century Bengal', *Past and Present*, vol. 86, pp. 121–48

Rushdie, S. 1982, *Midnight's Children*, 2nd edn, Picador/Pan Books, London

Russell, B. 1961, *History of Western Philosophy*, 2nd edn, George Allen & Unwin, London

Said, E. 1979, *The Question of Palestine*, Times Books, New York

——1981, *Covering Islam: How the Media and the Experts Determine How We See the Rest of the World*, Routledge & Kegan Paul, London

——1983, *The World, the Text and the Critic*, Harvard University Press, Cambridge, Massachusetts

——1986, 'Orientalism reconsidered', in *Literature, Politics & Theory*, eds. Barker et al., Methuen, London, pp. 210–29

——1989, 'Representing the colonized: anthropology's interlocutors', *Critical Inquiry*, vol. 15, no. 2, pp. 205–25

——1991 [1978], *Orientalism: Western Conceptions of the Orient*, 3rd edn, Penguin, Harmondsworth

——1993, *Culture and Imperialism*, Chatto & Windus, London

Sanchez, R. 1990, 'Ethnicity, ideology and academia', *Cultural Critique*, vol. 4, no. 3, pp. 294–302

Sandel, M. 1982, *Liberalism and the Limits of Justice*, Cambridge University Press, Cambridge

Sartre, Jean-Paul 1946, *Existentialism is a Humanism*, Nagel, Paris

——1969, *Being and Nothingness: An Essay on Phenomenological Ontology*, trans. Hazel E. Barnes, Methuen, London

Schiller, F. 1966, *On the Aesthetic Education of Man in a Series of Letters*, eds & trans. Elizabeth M. Wilkinson & L. A. Willoughby, Clarendon Press, Oxford

Seth, V. 1993, *A Suitable Boy*, Penguin Books/Viking, New Delhi

——1994 [1981], *Mappings*, 2nd edn Penguin Books/Viking, New Delhi

Sharpe, J. 1993, *Allegories of Empire: The Figure of Woman in the Colonial Text*, University of Minnesota Press, Minneapolis

Sheridan, S. 1990, 'Feminist knowledge, women's liberation, and women's studies', in *Feminist Knowledge: Critique and Construct*, ed. Sneja Gunew, Routledge, London pp. 36–58

Soyinka, W. 1996, *The Open Sore of A Continent: A Personal*

Narrative of the Nigerian Crisis, Oxford University Press, Oxford

Spanos, W. V. 1986, 'The Appolonian investment of modern humanist education: the examples of Matthew Arnold, Irving Babbit, and I. A. Richards', *Cultural Critique*, vol. 1, pp. 7–72

Spear, P. 1990, *A History of India: From the Sixteenth Century to the Twentieth Century*, vol. 2, 5th edn, Penguin, Harmondsworth

Spivak, G. 1985, 'Three women's texts and a critique of imperialism', *Critical Inquiry*, vol. 12, pp. 242–61

——1987, 'French feminism in an international frame', in *In Other Worlds: Essays in Cultural Politics*, Methuen, New York, pp. 134–53

——1988 [1985], 'Can the subaltern speak?', reprinted in *Marxist Interpretations of Culture*, eds Cary Nelson & Lawrence Grossberg, Macmillan Education, Basingstoke, pp. 271–313

——1990, *The Postcolonial Critic: Interviews, Strategies, Dialogues*, ed. Sarah Harasym, Routledge, New York

——1993, *Outside in the Teaching Machine*, Routledge, New York

Sprinker, M. (ed.) 1992, *Edward Said: A Critical Reader*, Blackwell, Oxford

Sri Aurobindo, 1991, *The Future Poetry*, 2nd edn, Sri Aurobindo Ashram Publication Department, Pondicherry

Suleri, S. 1992, *The Rhetoric of English India*, University of Chicago Press, Chicago

Talpade Mohanty, C. 1994, 'Under Western eyes: feminist scholarship and colonial discourse', reprinted in *Colonial Discourse and Postcolonial Theory: A Reader*, eds Patrick Williams & Laura Chrisman, Columbia University Press, New York, pp. 196–220

Taylor, C. 1975, *Hegel*, Cambridge University Press, Cambridge

Todorov, T. 1993, *On Human Diversity: Nationalism, Racism, and Exoticism in French Thought*, Harvard University Press, Cambridge, Massachusetts

Trinh T. Minh-ha 1989, *Woman, Native, Other*, Indiana University Press, Bloomington

——1991, *When the Moon Waxes Red: Representation, Gender and Cultural Politics*, Routledge, New York

Trivedi, H. 1993, *Colonial Transactions: English Literature and India*, Papyrus, Calcutta

Varadharajan, A. 1995, *Exotic Parodies: Subjectivity in Adorno, Said and Spivak*, University of Minnesota Press, Minneapolis

Viswanathan, G. 1989, *Masks of Conquest: Literary Studies and British Rule in India*, Faber & Faber, London

Warren, B. 1980, *Imperialism: Pioneer of Capitalism*, Verso, London

Weber, M. 1930, *The Protestant Ethic and the Spirit of Capitalism*, trans. Talcott Parsons, George Allen & Unwin, London

West, C. 1990, 'The new cultural politics of difference', *October*, vol. 53, pp. 93–109

White, J. 1993, 'Politics and the individual in the modernist historical novel: Gordimer and Rushdie', in *Recasting the World*, ed. Jonathan White, Johns Hopkins University Press, Baltimore, Maryland, pp. 208–40

White, J. (ed.) 1993, *Recasting the World: Writing After Colonialism*, The Johns Hopkins University Press, Baltimore, Maryland

Williams, P. & Chrisman, L. (eds) 1994, *Colonial Discourse and Postcolonial Theory: A Reader*, Columbia University Press, New York

Williams, R. 1981, *Culture*, Fontana, London

——1986, 'Forms of fiction in 1848' in *Literature, Politics and Theory*, eds Francis Barker et al., Methuen, London, pp. 1–16

'World Citizen' 1927, *Sister India: Critical Examination and a Reasoned Reply to Katherine Mayo's Mother India*

Woolf, V. 1992, *A Room of One's Own & Three Guineas*, ed. Morag Shiach, Oxford University Press, Oxford

Young, R. 1990, *White Mythologies: Writing History and the West*, Routledge, London

Index

cooperative venture,
123–5, 129–36, 138–9
postnational utopias, 82, 109,
125–9 *passim*, 136–40,
174–5
ethics of hybridity, 137–8
enlightened postnationalism,
124, 136
poststructuralism, 25, 131
analysis of power, 14–16
antagonistic relationship with
Marxism, 24–8, 74, 170
and Said's critique, 69–74
passim
critique of Western
epistemology, ix, 25–7, 30–1,
36–41 *passim*, 72
deconstruction, 159–60
power/knowledge link, 43, 48,
54–6, 64, 72–4
theoretical basis of
postcolonialism viii–ix, 25–7,
167
theorisation of cultural alterity,
ix, 14–16, 26, 31–2, 36–41,
72–3, 83
power, 37
coercive v. seductive, 14
double representation, 14–16
master–slave relationship, 16–22
passim, 111–12, 139
see also knowledge; Western
nationalism
Prakash, G., 15, 18, 134
Pratt, M. L., 125–6, 131, 133,
134–5
psychoanalysis, 8–10 *passim*, 78,
149
psychoanalytic feminism, 57
Purkayasta, S., 65

Ranger, T., 118
Rao, R., 150–1
rationalism *see* Cartesianism;
Enlightenment humanism
Rawls, J., 139–40
Reaganism, 69

religion, 104
Renaissance humanism
and German idealism, 50, 52
Arnold's totalitarian humanism,
50–2 *passim*
claims to disinterestedness, 45,
48, 50–1
concern with pedagogy, 29, 45
human-ness as content of
knowledge, 29, 42
humanism v. scholasticism, 47
origins, 42, 45–7, 49
production of whole or
representative human beings,
46, 48, 50
and capacity to command,
49–50
constraints on human-ness,
47–8
Homo humanus v. *Homo
barbarus*, 47–8
relation with the State, 50–1
collusion, 51–2, 55
flourishes where State under
threat, 51–2
moulding of ideal citizen
subjects, 49
State as proper end of
knowledge, 49, 50
role beyond the academy
extension of education, 46
political motivations, 48, 49,
50
studia humanitatis or liberal
arts, 45–52
exclusions of minor curricula
and social categories, 46–7,
51
umanista
academic monopoly, 45
forming and shaping role, 46,
48, 49
Rhodes, C., 169
Romanticism, 155, 160–2 *passim*,
165–6
Rousseau, J., 169

Index compiled by Geraldine Suter